Cambridge Elements ≡

Elements in Epistemology
edited by
Stephen Hetherington
University of New South Wales, Sydney

KNOWLEDGE-FIRST EPISTEMOLOGY

A Defence

Mona Simion
University of Glasgow

CAMBRIDGE
UNIVERSITY PRESS

Shaftesbury Road, Cambridge CB2 8EA, United Kingdom

One Liberty Plaza, 20th Floor, New York, NY 10006, USA

477 Williamstown Road, Port Melbourne, VIC 3207, Australia

314–321, 3rd Floor, Plot 3, Splendor Forum, Jasola District Centre,
New Delhi – 110025, India

103 Penang Road, #05–06/07, Visioncrest Commercial, Singapore 238467

Cambridge University Press is part of Cambridge University Press & Assessment,
a department of the University of Cambridge.

We share the University's mission to contribute to society through the pursuit of
education, learning and research at the highest international levels of excellence.

www.cambridge.org
Information on this title: www.cambridge.org/9781009454988

DOI: 10.1017/9781009454964

First published 2025

A catalogue record for this publication is available from the British Library

ISBN 978-1-009-45498-8 Hardback
ISBN 978-1-009-45499-5 Paperback
ISSN 2398-0567 (online)
ISSN 2514-3832 (print)

Knowledge-First Epistemology

A Defence

Elements in Epistemology

DOI: 10.1017/9781009454964
First published online: March 2025

Mona Simion
University of Glasgow

Author for correspondence: Mona Simion, mona.simion@glasgow.ac.uk

Abstract: Knowledge-first epistemology places knowledge at the normative core of epistemological affairs: on this approach, central epistemic phenomena are to be analysed in terms of knowledge. This Element offers a defence of an integrated, naturalistic knowledge-first account of justified belief, reasons, evidence and defeat, permissible assertion and action, and the epistemic normativity of practical and theoretical reasoning. On this account, *the epistemic* is an independent normative domain organized around one central etiological epistemic function: generating knowledge. In turn, this epistemic function generates epistemic norms of proper functioning that constitute the epistemic domain, and govern moves in our epistemic practice, such as forming beliefs, asserting, and reasoning. This title is also available as Open Access on Cambridge Core.

Keywords: knowledge-first epistemology, Timothy Williamson, knowledge norm of belief, knowledge norm of assertion, reasoning

ISBNs: 9781009454988 (HB), 9781009454995 (PB), 9781009454964 (OC)
ISSNs: 2398-0567 (online), 2514-3832 (print)

Contents

Introduction

Knowledge-first epistemology places knowledge at the normative core of epistemological affairs: on this approach, central epistemic phenomena are to be analysed in terms of knowledge. First put forth in the groundbreaking *Knowledge and Its Limits* (Williamson 2000), the knowledge-first approach to epistemological theorizing is one of the most successful and prolific research programmes in epistemology and philosophy in general, having given rise to novel theories of the epistemic justification ((Bird 2007), (Ichikawa 2014), (Lasonen-Aarnio MS), (Kelp 2016), (Millar 2010), (Miracchi 2015), (Schellenberg 2018), (Silva 2017), (Simion 2019), (Sutton 2005), (Williamson 2000)) the nature and normativity of evidence and defeat ((Lasonen-Aarnio 2014), (Kelp 2023), (Dutant & Littlejohn 2021), (Simion 2024c,d), (Williamson 2000)), understanding ((Kelp 2015), (Sliwa 2017)), the basing relation (Carter & Miracchi 2024), permissible suspension ((Miracchi 2017), (Simion 2024d)) norms of inquiry ((Kelp 2023), (Friedman 2020), (Willard-Kyle 2023)), rationality ((Dutant and Littlejohn Forthcoming), (Miracchi Forthcoming)), KK principles (Goodman and Salow 2018), epistemic functions ((Kelp 2018), (Simion 2019)), know-how and intentional action ((Pavese 2015), (Stanley & Williamson 2001)), epistemic responsibility and blame (Lasonen-Aarnio 2014, Williamson Forthcoming), norms of speech acts (Benton (2011), Kelp (2018), Kelp & Simion (2021), Simion (2021), Turri (2016), Williamson (1996)), action (Hawthorne & Stanley 2008), practical and theoretical reasoning ((Fantl & McGrath 2012), (Simion 2021), (Williamson 2000)), perceptual entitlement (Millar 2010, Schellenberg 2018), testimonial entitlement (Simion 2021), disagreement ((Hawthorne & Srinivasan 2013), (Simion & Broncano-Berrocal 2024)), group belief and group justification (Bird (2010), Simion, Carter, and Kelp (2022)), the epistemology of science (Bird 2022) and the epistemology of law (Bloome-Tillmann 2017, Littlejohn 2017, Moss 2019).

Claims paradigmatically associated with the knowledge-first programme include that knowledge is a mental state, that it is unanalysable, that it is distinctively valuable, that knowledge is the aim of inquiry and belief formation, that other epistemic normative phenomena (e.g. justification, understanding, responsibility, evidence, defeat) are to be unpacked in terms of knowledge, that knowledge is the norm of assertion and action, that it is essential to intentional action, that social epistemic phenomena (e.g. testimony, disagreement, group belief) afford unpacking in terms of knowledge. Crucially, many of these claims are theoretically independent from each-other; unsurprisingly, while some knowledge-first theorists subscribe to the full research programme, others only champion some of its claims.

This study focuses on the normative core of the programme: it offers a defence of an integrated, naturalistic knowledge-first account of justified belief, reasons, evidence, and defeat, permissible assertion and action, and the epistemic normativity of practical and theoretical reasoning. On this account, *the epistemic* is an independent normative domain organized around one central function – knowledge – which generates epistemic norms.

Here is the game plan: in Section 1, I argue that the main epistemic etiological function of our epistemic practice of inquiry is generating knowledge. In turn, this epistemic function generates epistemic norms governing moves in our epistemic practice, such as forming and maintaining beliefs, asserting, and reasoning. Section 2 discusses the epistemic normativity of belief and the nature of justification. Section 3 integrates the account of justification with a theory of the nature and normativity of reasons, evidence, and defeat. Section 4 discusses the normativity of action and assertion, and Section 5 defends a unified account of epistemically good reasoning.

1 The Knowledge Function

Introduction

Tim Williamson (2000) famously argues for the knowledge-first programme on abductive grounds: the best explanation for the fact that an analysis of knowledge has proven elusive for several decades is that knowledge does not afford a non-circular dismantling analysis. If so, we should use knowledge as a primitive in analysing other central epistemic phenomena.

This section's ambition is to offer further support to the knowledge-first programme. I argue that generating knowledge is the function of our epistemic practices, and that this function generates epistemic norms of proper functioning that constitute the epistemic domain.

1.1 Knowledge Is the Function of Inquiry

What is the function of our epistemic practice of inquiry? A clarification: In asking this question, I follow tradition[1] and speak of inquiry broadly conceived: that is, I take all of our epistemic endeavours to fall under the general epistemic practice of inquiry: automatically formed attitudes (beliefs that I form as I walk down the street) as well as careful reasonings and judgments, suspensions,

---

[1] E.g. Kelp (2014a, 2021), Sosa (2023).

credence formations, as well as epistemic exchanges – assertions, tellings, conjectures, and so on.

Inquiry is an epistemic practice. Practices have main intrinsic goals, or functions: the practice of driving mainly aims at safely getting one to one's destination in a reasonable amount of time; that's its main function. The practice of cooking mainly aims at producing tasty and nutritious food. The practice of medicine aims at generating health, and so on. The restriction to intrinsic here is crucial; often, but less importantly for my purposes here, practices have extrinsic aims too. Plausibly, the practice of inquiry and the practice of medicine share their extrinsic aim: the aim of survival. Compatibly with that, these two practices will have different intrinsic aims. Ideally, when the intrinsic aim of the practice is achieved, it reliably serves the achievement of the corresponding extrinsic aim. This, however, may not be the case. Some of our practices are bad for us.

Now, note that, when it comes to their goals, practices tend to strike a good balance between value and achievability; they are often aimed at the most valuable achievable intrinsic goal. The value at stake is not good *simpliciter*, to be sure; many of our practices have horrible goals! What is at stake is domain-specific goodness. Driving does not aim at teleporting you to your destination. Nor does it aim at safely getting you one mile away from your destination. It aims at getting you to your destination – which is the most valuable target in the domain – in a reasonable amount of time – which is an achievable goal. Similarly, cooking aims at producing tasty food, not at producing, say, self-generating nutrients (not achievable), nor half-baked goods (not the most valuable). Medicine aims at generating health, not at making us immortal (not achievable) nor at keeping us barely alive (not the most valuable goal). Practices' intrinsic goals tend to strike a good balance between value and achievability.

It is widely accepted that knowledge is, epistemically, more valuable than any lesser epistemic standing. The way in which knowledge is more valuable has been a topic of debate in the past years (e.g. Pritchard (2010)). The challenge, however, is to explain how, not to argue that it is: little doubt[2] has there been expressed – since Plato's *Meno* – with regard to the superiority in value thesis itself. Furthermore, several people think that knowledge is not only more valuable than lesser epistemic standings, but also distinctively so. That is, the difference is one in kind rather than in degree (Pritchard 2010, Simion and Kelp 2019). I have argued in previous work that this is so because knowledge marks a jump on the epistemic value continuum, in that it stands in a non-Archimedean

---

[2] But see e.g. Pritchard (2009) and Kvanvig (2003) on scepticism about the value of knowledge.

value relation to states that fall short of knowledge: for the aim of leading a cognitively flourishing life, for creatures like us, some amount of knowledge is better than any amount of mere true beliefs. A life of cognitive flourishing is a life rich (enough) in knowledge.

Second, note that, in most epistemic walks of life, knowledge is readily available (Kelp & Simion 2017): we are fairly well-equipped epistemic agents, living in an extremely friendly epistemic environment. Furthermore, knowledge is much more readily available, and thus much more easily achievable, than both lesser and stronger epistemic standings. When it comes to stronger states – such as certainty or understanding –, that should be easy to see. It takes us quite a bit of time and effort – and, arguably, a fair amount of knowledge – to achieve understanding. Furthermore, (epistemic) certainty is hard.

To see it for states that fall short of knowledge too, consider first perceptual beliefs about middle-sized dry goods. My belief that there is a computer on the desk before me qualifies as knowledge: it is produced by a highly reliable ability to recognize computers in an epistemically hospitable environment. The crucial point is that belief formation by suitable processes in hospitable environments is the norm; formation of beliefs by unsuitable process, or in inhospitable environments is the exception. If this isn't immediately clear, consider again my belief that there is a computer on the desk before me and ask yourself what would have to be the case for my belief to remain true but fall short of knowledge: I mistake a hologram for a computer, whilst unbeknownst to me there is a computer somewhere else on the desk, I acquire my belief by a highly unreliable process such as a coin-toss. While any of this might come to pass, it is undeniable that, as a matter of fact, it only rarely does.

Consider, also, testimonial belief about propositions of practical importance: propositions about bills that need to be paid, the nature of your sickness and the medication that will cure it, what's available at the local restaurant, and so on. Or consider inferentially supported beliefs that exploit a variety of natural and social regularities: that my couch is still in my living room, that Paris is still the capital of France, and so on. Here too, when beliefs in these ranges are formed by suitable processes in sufficiently hospitable epistemic environments, they will qualify as knowledge.

These considerations suggest that, in a wide range of cases, knowledge is easily achievable. All we have to do to acquire knowledge is open our eyes, listen to what other people tell us, attend to our feelings, and so on. In contrast, true belief that falls short of knowledge is a rare commodity that exists only in very special environments. What is readily available is true belief *that is* knowledge (Kelp & Simion 2017).

Why not say that the aim of belief is truth (not true belief that falls short of knowledge, but truth *simpliciter*)? If we aim at true beliefs, every instance of knowledge will accomplish this aim, and so will some true beliefs that aren't knowledge. So true beliefs will be an easier aim to achieve than knowledge. Furthermore, plausibly, in the vast majority of cases, true belief just is knowledge.[3]

If I am right and the goal of a practice is often defined by the best score on both achievability and value, however, in virtue of the distinctive value of knowledge, knowledge and not true belief is plausibly the goal of the practice, even if the latter is present whenever the former is present and, sometimes (but not often) when the former is absent. To see this, note that, similarly, getting one to one's destination is more plausibly the goal of driving than getting one to a point that's situated precisely one inch before one's destination, in virtue of the fact that the former is more valuable than the latter (in spite of the fact that the latter is always achieved when the former is, and, likely, in virtue of being more easily achievable, on some cases when the former is not).

To take stock: We have seen that goals of practices tend to strike a good balance between value and achievability: they are the most valuable achievable goals. I have argued that knowledge is more valuable than lesser epistemic standings and much more easily achievable than both weaker and stronger states.

I submit, in the light of all this, that we have good reason to believe that knowledge is the most valuable achievable epistemic state, and thus *the* function of the epistemic practice of inquiry.

Importantly, that is not to say that some particular species of inquiry can't aim at stronger epistemic states: to the contrary, it is plausible that, for instance, scientific and moral inquiry aim at understanding the relevant phenomena. Note, though, that this is perfectly compatible with our general practice of inquiry aiming at knowledge, since species of a genus are bound to have extra-properties, on top of those of the genus itself.[4]

Perhaps more surprisingly, my view is also compatible with a particular species of inquiry aiming at less than knowledge. Here is why: a well-researched category in normative ethics is that of 'contrary-to-duty imperatives'. Very roughly, these are norms that step in when one is in breach of a norm. You break your neighbour's window; that is in violation of quite a few types of norms – moral, social, prudential, and so on. Now, the contrary-to-duty

---

[3] See also Hetherington (2000) for a view that uses a similar claim to put forth an analysis of knowledge as true belief.

[4] I am assuming a view on which understanding implies knowledge (see e.g. Kelp (2015)). For non-factive views of understanding, see e.g. Elgin (2017).

imperative asks you to apologize: it's what one ought to do given that not breaking the norm is not an option that's still on the table. It's the next best thing to do.

Similarly, there are domains where and situations when knowledge is not attainable. Some think philosophy is a domain like that;[5] I disagree. However, if this is true, we should expect this sub-domain of inquiry to be aimed at less than knowledge – roughly, to be aimed at the next best epistemic standing. Alternatively, one might be in a situation where urgency makes it unlikely that knowledge is achievable in the available amount of time: reporting is often like that. In these situations, as I have argued at length elsewhere,[6] one's reporting should be based on the best achievable epistemic standing. Again, all this is perfectly compatible with the framework I am developing here.[7]

1.2 Etiological Functions

I borrow the general normative picture I rely on from philosophy of biology – that is, from the normativity of etiological functions: in traits, artefacts and practices alike, functions generate norms. There is such a thing as a properly functioning heart, a properly functioning can opener and a proper way to make coffee. If that is so, what we need in order to identify a particular type of norm governing a particular type of practice, is to first identify its function.

---

[5] See e.g. Goldberg (2017).

[6] Simion 2016.

[7] Crucially, note that this observation (in conjunction with the value-theoretic picture defended so far) leaves it open whether in these fields, belief that falls short of knowledge will be permissible: after all, one need not hold that one should always end inquiry with belief: justified credence might do. Furthermore, what one wants to say here will also depend on one's commitments concerning justified belief and suspension. For people liking the claim that justified belief is knowledge, suspension will be permissible only when one does not have enough epistemic support for knowledge (e.g. Hawthorne and Srinivasan 2013). On my preferred view (Simion 2024d), suspension is justified insofar as one does not have the support needed for forming a justified belief, and justified belief is belief formed via a properly functioning knowledge-generating cognitive capacity (see Section 2). Views like this might raise some eyebrows (see e.g. McGlynn 2014): say that I know that I cannot know that p, but I also know that I have pretty strong support for p (just not enough for knowledge). Lottery cases are paradigmatic cases in this respect. Why should I not believe? After all, a true belief is surely more valuable than suspension. Note, however, that (1) just because belief is also epistemically valuable, it does not yet follow that it is more valuable than suspension, and (2) views like these do not predict that full neutrality is required in these cases – but mere belief suspension: one can always form the corresponding credence, without seemingly missing out on much. A high credence that one's preferred philosophical theory is true seems to be sufficient to get by, without full belief on the topic. For arguments against the Lockean thesis (i.e. the thesis that justified belief maps on to sufficient justification for high credence short of 1), see e.g. Kelp (2014b) and Douven and Williamson (2006).

On the etiological theory of functions,[8] functions turn on histories that explain why the item exists or operates the way it does. Take my heart: tokens of the type pumped blood in my ancestors. This was beneficial for my ancestors' survival, which explains why tokens of the type continue to exist. As a result, my heart acquired the etiological function (henceforth also e-function) of pumping blood. Acquiring an etiological function is a success story: traits, artefacts and actions get etiological functions of a particular type by producing the relevant type of benefit. My heart acquired a biological etiological function by generating biological benefit. Through a positive feedback mechanism – the heart pumped blood, which kept the organism alive, which, in turn, ensured the continuous existence of the heart – our hearts acquired the etiological function of pumping blood.

Not all functional items follow the model of the heart: there will be cases where a requirement of selection over generations for function acquisition will be implausibly strong.[9] The paradigmatic case is that of beneficial macro-mutations, also known as hopeful monsters[10] (Graham 2014, 30). Most mutations are harmful (think of extreme birth defects); once in a while, though, a happy accident happens: someone is born with an almost entirely new trait or organ, very different in kind from its ancestral trait, which actually benefits the recipient. Since they are mutations, they don't have an evolutionary history; they are 'first generation' traits. Still, they can acquire functions. What matters is that the existence/continuous existence of a trait is explained via a history of positive feedback.

While etiology does require some history, then, it does not require an awful lot of it; there are several ways to cash out the etiological requirement that do not presuppose directional selection, that is, selection over generations.[11] A trait can also acquire a particular function by ongoing, maintenance selection, or through a learning process, or even by the metabolic activity of the organism itself. What it all amounts to is explaining the existence/continuous existence of a trait through a longer or shorter history of positive feedback (Graham 2014, 35).

Here is, then, on a first approximation, what it takes for a trait to have an etiological function of a particular type:

E-Function: A token of type T has the e-function of type B of producing effect E in system S iff (1) tokens of T produced E in the past, (2) producing E resulted

---

[8] Defended by e.g. David J. Buller (1998), Ruth Millikan (1984), Karen Neander (1991). The etiological theory of functions is, by far, the most widely endorsed view in the literature. Its main competitor is the systemic theory of functions defended in Cummins (1975).

[9] See e.g. Sosa (1993) on Swampman.

[10] Davidson's Swampman is the epistemic incarnation thereof (Sosa 1993).

[11] See Buller (1998) for an excellent overview of etiological theories of function.

in benefit of type B in S or S's ancestors and (3) producing E's having B-benefitted S or S's ancestors contributes to the explanation of why T continues to exist in S.

Importantly, in contrast to orthodoxy (Graham (2012), Millikan (1984)), which takes biological benefit to ground all etiological functions, my account takes functions to be typed by the corresponding benefit. As such, on my account, if a trait produces a benefit of type B in a system, the function thereby acquired will be a function of type B. If it is biological benefit that is at stake in function acquisition, what we get is a biological function. On this view, the heart's function to pump blood is a biological function in virtue of the fact that the produced benefit is also biological – that is, survival. The function of music is an aesthetic function in virtue of the fact that the produced benefit is an aesthetic benefit. And so on. Now, of course, aesthetic benefit might, and often will, also result in biological benefit. When this happens, music will also thereby acquire a biological function. What is important to keep in mind, though, is that the benefit that is *essential* to aesthetic function acquisition is the aesthetic one. The fact that biological benefit is also associated with it is, at best, a contingent matter of fact.

The etiological functionalist picture offers further support to the knowledge-function hypothesis. To see this, note that knowledge meets E-Function:

E-Function-Inquiry: The practice of inquiry has the epistemic e-function of generating knowledge in the population iff (1) inquiry has produced knowledge in the past, (2) producing knowledge resulted in epistemic benefit in the population and (3) the fact that (2) contributes to the explanation of why the practice of inquiry persists in the population.

(1) is overwhelmingly plausible on pain of generalized scepticism: our practice of inquiry has produced knowledge in the past; (2) is the widely accepted distinctive epistemic value of knowledge thesis; finally, plausibly, the fact that it was successful in generating knowledge contributes to the explanation why our practice of inquiry has not been discontinued (3).

If this is the case, it follows that knowledge is, at least, *one* epistemic function of inquiry. That is enough for it to generate corresponding epistemic norms.

Of course, knowledge is not the *only* epistemic state that meets the E-function: a case could be made for thinking that producing true beliefs, justified beliefs, certainty, understanding meets the E-function for inquiry. Why not, then, think that one function of inquiry is to produce knowledge, another is to produce true beliefs, another is to produce justified beliefs, another is to produce understanding, and so on? And if this picture is plausible, why think knowledge is 'first' in the relevant sense – in that we should analyse all other epistemically interesting phenomena in terms of knowledge – rather than have a pluralistic picture, where the epistemic domain is organized around several epistemic goods, which deliver distinct epistemic norms?[12]

Lots of things have several functions of different types: clothing, for instance, serves a prudential function (keeping us warm), and an aesthetic function (generating good aesthetic experiences). Each of these types of function will generate corresponding types of norms: prudential functions will generate prudential norms, aesthetic functions will generate aesthetic norms, and so on. Sometimes, however, things can serve several functions of the same type (T-function). When this happens, the question that arises is: which T-function is the one generating the norms governing the thing in question? The answer is: the main T-function (Simion 2019). To see this, note that the main T-function of a trait is the one that maps on to attributive goodness (Geach 1956), and thus to meeting the corresponding evaluative norm: the one that determines when something is a good token of its type. For instance, the main prudential function of a knife is to cut things. We know this because it maps on to what it is for a knife to be a good token of its type: a good knife is a sharp knife. Blunt knives can also serve secondary prudential functions; for instance, they may be useful for kids playing house, or for being displayed in a museum. Compatibly, what determines attributive goodness is the main function of the knife.

Why think that knowledge is *the main* function of inquiry? Why not truth, for instance? Since knowledge is a stronger epistemic standing than truth, arguing from the claim that generating knowledge is *one* epistemic function of inquiry to the stronger claim that the main function is generating knowledge rather than truth will be fairly straightforward. After all, knowledge implies truth; if pumping blood in our circulatory system is one biological function of the heart, it will be fairy implausible to hold that, alongside this particular function, the heart also has the function of pumping.

Note, also, that what the case of the heart suggests is that proper function ascriptions are value loaded: that is, the proper description of the function corresponds to the (most) valuable contribution of the respective trait to the relevant system. The function is pumping blood in the circulatory system – not just pumping blood, since pumping it anywhere else would fail to be valuable for the organism; also, not just pumping *something* in the circulatory system, since pumping orange juice would also fail to do the work. On the other hand, the function of the heart is not 'pumping blood and making a beating sound' either; plausibly, that is because pumping blood and making a beating sound

---

[12] E.g. Gerken (2018) resists knowledge-first and proposes a pluralistic picture along these lines.

does not seem to be in any way more valuable to the organism than merely pumping blood. If that is the case, however, it looks as though, similarly to the case of the heart, value considerations give us reason to believe that proper function attribution involves knowledge rather than true belief.

How about certainty or understanding? Will these states not be more valuable than knowledge? And if so, will they not be good candidates for being the main function of inquiry?[13] Two things about this: first, many think these states just amount to knowledge (e.g. Williamson 2000, Khalifa 2017, Kelp 2015, Sliwa 2017).[14] Second, for theorists that deny this, E-Function will be hard to defend for their preferred epistemic states: if certainty is a stronger epistemic state than knowledge (something like Cartesian certainty, perhaps), there is a worry that limited cognizers like us have not achieved it much in the past, in which case it does not meet E-Function. Conversely, people who deny that understanding reduces to knowledge usually hold a non-factive account. If so, the claim that understanding is more valuable than knowledge, and thus the main E-Function of inquiry, is rather implausible (or at least in need of further defence).[15]

1.3 Epistemic Functions and Epistemic Norms

I have argued that generating knowledge is the epistemic etiological function of inquiry. If this is right, we have all we need to move on to identifying central epistemic norms that we are interested in.

Here is why: epistemically significant endeavours such as forming beliefs, judging, asserting, and reasoning are moves in the practice of inquiry. Moves in practices aim (either directly or indirectly) to fulfil the function of the practice. The difference between direct and indirect aiming lies with achievability: for some moves in practices, the goal of the practice is only indirectly rather than

---

[13] E.g. Falbo (2023) and Woodard (forthcoming) argue that inquiry sometimes aims at a more demanding status than knowledge. Beddor (2020) argues that many of our epistemic practices are geared around epistemic certainty. Nado (2019) argues that much of scientific practice is geared primarily at securing an epistemic state that reduces the chance of error well below the threshold usually required for knowledge.

[14] In the case of objectual understanding, many theorists believe it amounts to something like comprehensive and interconnected knowledge (e.g. Kelp 2015, Sliwa 2017). As such, objectual understanding will plausibly be the function of inquiry into general phenomena, rather than into questions of fact – and thus will not compete with the claim defended here.

[15] Does all this tell us that we have to take knowledge – and only knowledge – as primitive in epistemology? Do these considerations imply the implausibility of an epistemic pluralistic picture? No, more work will have to be done to this effect – work that falls outside of the ambitions (and available space) here. This section provides positive arguments in support of the plausibility of a knowledge-first picture, rather than knock-down arguments against an alternative methodological approach. Compatibly, everyone has to choose their primitive(s), and at the end of the day, the methodological approach that fares best in terms of theoretical virtues of the resulting theory will be the preferable theory. This Element makes the case for putting knowledge first.

directly reachable. Diabetological consults are moves in the practice of medicine, and they aim directly at fulfilling the goal of the practice of medicine: curing diseases. In turn, some moves aim at this final practice goal only indirectly, while aiming directly at intermediate goals: performing glycemia tests aims (directly) at informing the diabetologist as to how well the patient is doing, which, in turn, aims directly at her diagnosing the patient correctly, and, further, at curing her disease. In this, glycemia tests aim indirectly at the goal of the practice of medicine. They aim at making progress towards it. Baking cakes is a move in the practice of cooking, and it aims directly at fulfilling the aim of the practice: producing tasty, nourishing food. My getting the flour off the shelf aims indirectly at the general aim of the practice by aiming directly at adding flour to the cake mix. It aims at making progress towards producing tasty, nourishing food. And so on.

Similarly, moves in the practice of inquiry – that is, all epistemically significant states and actions – will aim either directly – plausibly: belief formation, assertions, reasonings – or indirectly: credences, withholdings, suspensions – at the aim of the practice of inquiry. The difference, again, will lie with goal achievability. Since beliefs, assertions and conclusions of reasonings can be knowledgeable, in a way in which things like credences, suspensions, and withholdings cannot, we get a picture whereby belief formation aims directly at fulfilling the function of the practice of inquiry (knowledge), while, at the same time, credence forming, suspending, and withholding aim at knowledge indirectly: the formation of these transitional attitudes aims directly at adjusting ones doxastic states to the available evidence, which, in turn, plausibly ultimately aims at the aim of inquiry – knowledge generation.[16]

The etiological account is an account of functions as purposes: by being selected for it, our hearts have acquired the purpose of pumping blood in our organisms. Reaching that purpose – that is, successfully pumping blood – will amount to function fulfilment. But purposes will also come with associated norms prescribing the right way to proceed in order to reliably enough reach the corresponding purpose in normal conditions. Because its function contributes to the explanation of its very existence, the trait in question *ought* to perform in a way that is associated with likely function fulfilment in normal conditions – that is, conditions similar to those in which it was selected. Your heart will be properly functioning when it will work in the way in which it reliably enough fulfils its function of pumping blood in your circulatory system in normal conditions: beating at rate of 60–120 beats per minute when resting.

---

[16] This Element will not discuss norms for transitional attitudes. See Staffel (Forthcoming) for a book-length treatment, Kelp and Simion (2024) for credences and Simion (2024d) for proper suspension.

Note, then, that there are two ways a functional item might go right, and two ways it may go wrong. The unhappy cases are: breach of the norm of proper function, that is, malfunction (in the case of the heart, not beating at the relevant rate) and failure to fulfil its function (not pumping blood). The happy scenarios are, of course, proper functioning (beating at the relevant rate) and function fulfilment (pumping blood). Crucially, failure/success in one respect need not imply failure/success in the other. A trait can be malfunctioning – thus, in breach of the norm – and still fulfil its function (i.e. reach its aim), and the other way around: proper functioning need not imply function fulfilment. To see this, think of a situation where a surgeon takes the heart out of your chest, places it in a vat full of nutrients for a short while and plugs it to a pipe circuit filled with orange juice (Graham 2012, 449). Your heart, of course, will fail to fulfil its function of pumping blood under these circumstances; it will, as a matter of fact, be pumping orange juice. But this does not make it into a malfunctioning heart; to see this, compare it to a heart that has stopped pumping blood because it has been stabbed by a dagger.

Also, not only need proper functioning not imply function fulfilment, but the other direction of the entailment does not hold either. After all, your dagger-stabbed heart can fulfil its function in spite of being malfunctioning, through some lucky circumstance, say, a blood circulation-triggering magnetic field of sorts being in place.

Let us take stock: the etiological theory of functions gives a respectable naturalistic gloss to norms and purposes: your heart aims at pumping blood because successfully reaching this aim contributes to its continuous existence. Also, your heart ought to beat at a particular rate, because that is the way in which it reliably enough fulfils its function.

It turns out, then, that the e-functionalist picture constitutes itself in a straightforward norm-identification machinery. First, we need to identify the e-function served by the trait/artefact/practice in question. Once the function is identified, the question we need to ask ourselves is: how does the trait/artefact/practice fulfil its function in normal conditions? The answer to this question will give us proper functioning. In turn, the relevant trait/artefact/practice will be functioning permissibly if and only if it is properly functioning; like this, we get the content of the norm we are after.

Furthermore, on this picture, we also get an easy way to identify the type of norm at stake: norms will be typed by the corresponding functions, which, in turn, are typed by the produced benefit.

This way to think about epistemic normativity has three main advantages: first, it is naturalistically respectable. Second, it delivers normative independence for epistemology from other normative domains: the epistemic practice of inquiry is organized around an intrinsic epistemic value: knowledge. Third, importantly, the account neatly integrates the normativity of all epistemically significant endeavours as dropping out of the knowledge function of inquiry.

One worry that I hear sometimes is that functionalist norms may not be normatively 'oomph-y' enough to play the roles that epistemologists are interested in. Particular types of functions will deliver particular types of norms, independently on whether function fulfilment is all-things-considered valuable. There will be practices among assassins that have certain functions. Are these genuine values/norms at all? Don't functionalist norms suffer from lack of 'normative oomph'?[17]

Central values in a domain are valuable for their own sake, *relative to the domain*. It is a different question altogether, however, whether the domain itself is of any independent value to begin with. Some norms in some domains will have further normative *oomph* (not merely domain restricted, that is), insofar as the domain itself is valuable. For the epistemic domain, the question of 'normative oomph' is, then: is the domain itself valuable to begin with – which in turn, would give non-domain-specific normative oomph to its internal norms – or not?

On my account, epistemic norms have (1) domain-bound normative force, in that they promote knowledge, which is the value around which the domain is organized, and (2) not-domain-bound normative force, in that 'the epistemic' is a domain that is valuable for our survival. I find it empirically plausible that the reason why our cognitive capacities continue to exist is because they are good for us, biologically. Importantly, though, on my account, epistemic normativity *does not reduce* to biological normativity. Epistemic normativity is there to 'serve' epistemic functions alone. Compatibly, fulfilled epistemic functions are *de facto* good for us, biologically, and thus epistemic norms also enjoy non-domain-specific normative *oomph* because doing well epistemically is, at least for the most part, good for us, biologically.

Conclusion

I have argued that knowledge is the main etiological epistemic function of inquiry. Furthermore, I have shown that, once we have identified the epistemic function of the practice of inquiry, this will give us epistemic norms of proper functioning governing moves in the practice, such as belief formation, reasonings, and speech acts: it will give us a full knowledge-first theory of epistemic normativity. The following sections develop this theory.

---

[17] Thanks to Matt McGrath for very inspiring discussions on this topic.

2 Justified Belief

Introduction

Justification is widely taken to be normative. The following is an attractive way of capturing this thought:

The Deontic Thesis (DT). One's φ-ing is *prima facie* practically, morally, epistemically, and so on justified if and only if one *prima facie* practically, morally, epistemically, and so on permissibly φs.

If DT captures the way in which justification is normative, then DTB captures the sense in which the epistemic justification of belief is normative:

The Deontic Thesis for Belief (DTB). One's belief that p is *prima facie* epistemically justified if and only if one epistemically *prima facie* permissibly believes that p.[18]

Given a substantive account of permissible belief, we can use DTB to derive a substantive account of justified belief and vice versa.

2.1 Simple Knowledge-First Theories of Justification

Here is one popular account of the normativity of belief:

KNB: A belief is epistemically permissible if and only if knowledgeable.

DTB in conjunction with KNB gives:

JB=K: One's belief that p is epistemically justified if and only if knowledgeable.

Several philosophers follow Tim Williamson (2000) in upholding both KNB and JB=K (e.g. Littlejohn (2013), Sutton (2005)). The view has important theoretical advantages: it predicts lack of justification in cases featuring beliefs based on bare statistical evidence: these are cases of lack of knowledge, therefore lack of justification. It neatly explains historical failures to offer a dismantling analysis of knowledge; it delivers a unified normative picture for belief, assertion, reasoning, and action: on this picture, knowledge is the unique epistemic norm.

JB=K faces one important worry,[19] however:[20] on JB=K, the concept of justification seems too strong to play some of the most important roles we

---

[18] I will use 'justification' as shorthand for 'epistemic justification', unless otherwise specified.

[19] Some authors have challenged the knowledge norm of belief on linguistic grounds, that is, on the grounds that it conflicts with the way we use 'belief' in language to hedge; see, for example, van Elswyk & Willard Kyle (forthcoming).

[20] See e.g. McGlynn (2014) and Brown (2018).

have historically wanted it to play: it fails to grant justification to both deceived and Gettierized victims[21] – after all, they don't know – and it fails to allow for justified false beliefs.

That being said, of course, knowledge-firsters are not known to be particularly worried about being in line with tradition – and the traditional, non-factive notion of justification doesn't make an exception. Compatibly, however, anyone who wants to offer an extensionally adequate theory needs to either accommodate the intuitions of the traditionalist, or else offer a convincing error theory.

Traditionally, JB=K theorists distinguish between blameworthiness and norm violation to answer this worry. According to them, we are not very good at distinguishing between intuitions pertaining to these two different normative categories; the 'warm and fuzzy feeling' that we get when we consider the unfortunate epistemic situation of, for instance, the deceived victim (or the Gettierized victim, or the epistemically conscientious false believer), we confuse for approval sourced in compliance with the norm of belief, when, in fact, its source is mere blameless norm violation.[22]

Now, since blamelessness is, itself, a normative notion, there are conditions – that is, normative constraints – that one needs to meet in order to qualify as a blameless norm violator. Here are but a few identified in the relevant literature: lack of control over one's actions, ignorance ((Kelp and Simion 2017), (Littlejohn Forthcoming), (Zimmerman 1997)), being generally disposed to conform with the norm, acting as one who is so disposed (Williamson Forthcoming). The question, then, becomes: what is the status of these further constraints?

According to Tim Williamson, these normative constraints are derivative of the primary norm at stake – the knowledge norm of belief (Forthcoming, 7–8). On this normatively pluralist picture, there is an important difference to be made between the normative status conferred by the primary norm governing φ-ing – mapping on to justified φ-ing – and the normative status conferred by mere compliance with the derivative norms – mapping on to blameless norm violating φ-ing. In this way, according to Williamson, the deceived, the Gettierized victim, and the conscientious false believer, while doing what someone disposed to comply with the norm of belief would do – and thereby complying with the blamelessness-conferring derivative norm – they fail to comply with the primary, justification-conferring norm.

---

[21]　See Gettier (1963) and Goldman (1976).
[22]　Littlejohn (Forthcoming), Williamson (Forthcoming).

Insofar as it is overwhelmingly plausible that, in general, norms can be blamelessly broken, the JB=K line drops out nicely from general normativity theory.[23]

There are two worries for this move, though. The first pertains to the account's potential to capture all the needed normative distinctions. The problem cases are cases in which cognizers employ bad methods of belief formation (e.g. astrology) blamelessly, because they don't know better (nor could they have known better). There intuitively seems to be an epistemically interesting normative distinction between deceived and Gettierized victims, or everyday conscientious false believers on one hand, and believers blamelessly and unbeknownst to them employing epistemically dubious methods in forming beliefs on the other. The former are intuitively epistemically better off than the latter. If I falsely believe the train is leaving at 8 because that's what the website of the rail company shows, one might think, I am epistemically superior to someone who (unbeknownst to them) forms the same belief based on wishful thinking. However, on a picture like JB=K, it's hard to see why, since all these cases are predicted to be cases of blamelessness.

Second, note that epistemology is not strange in the normative landscape for needing a distinction between justification/permissibility on one hand, and success on the other. Giving money to charity is a morally justified/permissible action even if, on a particular occasion, due to a strike of bad luck, the money fails to reach its intended target, and thus your action is not successful in helping people. However, on the JB=K knowledge-first picture, successful belief and justified/permissible belief coincide: they both amount to knowledgeable belief. This turns the concept of epistemic justification in a bit of an odd ball in the normative landscape; for prior plausibility, the JB=K theorist owes us an explanation as to why this should be so.

2.2 Modal Knowledge-First Theories of Justification

In response to worries along the previous lines, several more complex knowledge-first views have been put forth in the literature. The recipe is, again, normative pluralism: recall that Williamson took the primary norm of belief (the knowledge norm) to map on to justification, while derivative norms to map on to blamelessness. Contra JB=K, complex views take the permissibility at stake in DTB to map on to milder, non-factive norms.

To see how this goes, note that DTB makes no mention of what norm the permissibility mapping on to justification refers to. Of course, if there is one and

---

[23] For worries, see Gerken (2011) and Brown (2018).

only one norm of belief, the answer is easy. On a normative pluralist picture, however, what we need is a more restricted version of DTB, that makes it clear to what norm the permissibility at stake refers to. One need not abandon either KNB or DTB. One can just go for normative pluralism in conjunction with a different, milder epistemic norm featured in DTB. On this type of view, while knowledge is *the evaluative* norm of belief – for what a good belief is – justification will map on to permissibility by a weaker (often derivative, prescriptive) norm governing belief.

There are several families of views in the literature developed along these lines.

One such account is the modal account. According to Alexander Bird (2004), Jonathan Ichikawa (2014), and Steven Reynolds (2013), justification is (in a sense to be specified further), would-be-knowledge: it maps on to some features of the believer, which, in conjunction with friendlier external conditions, would constitute knowledge.

For Bird, what matters is that the believer have the same mental states at this world as a knower does at a different possible world (Bird 2007, 86). According to Jonathan Ichikawa, 'a subject's belief is justified just in case her intrinsic state is consistent with her having knowledge' (2014, 189). Finally, Reynolds imposes a (non-stringent) accessibilst condition on justification: on his account, justification is the appearance of knowledge (2013, 369).

Recall that we have seen that, when it comes to justification in general, successful φ-ing comes apart from justified φ-ing. Modal knowledge-first views vindicate this thought, and thus score better than JB=K on this front. According to its champions, knowledge is the goal of belief – as such, successful belief will be knowledgeable belief – while the permissibility at stake in DTB maps on to a weaker state: would-be-knowledge.

The question that naturally arises for these views, however, is one of prior plausibility: why should we think would-be-knowledge has the normative significance ascribed to it by these views? The champions of modal accounts give different answers to this question.

Reynolds takes the normativity of assertion to explain the normative status of possible knowledge. According to him, knowledge is the norm of assertion, and one needs to keep one's beliefs in constant check for assertability. Awareness of knowledge, then, is instrumental to permissible assertion, which explains its distinctive normative status (Reynolds 2013, 367). There are two main worries for this move, however: First, assertion is a social phenomenon. Surely, though, we already had justified beliefs before living in a society. Second, for Reynolds's argument to work, what is needed is a fairly sophisticated second order state of awareness. That is, quite a bit of reflective work and conceptual competence seem needed for selecting assertable beliefs; this makes the view unfriendly towards non-sophisticated cognizers. Surely, though, my three-year-old daughter Mia is justified to believe that there is milk in the fridge, in spite of her incompetence in assessing beliefs for assertability.

Ichikawa identifies a different normative source: he takes matters internal to the believer to map on to blamelessness. According to him, then, justified belief is a kind of blameless belief, which explains its normative significance (Ichikawa 2014, 193). Recall, though, that one important worry for JB=K was that the account predicted no normative difference between massively deceived and Gettierized victims, or everyday conscientious false believers on one hand, and believers blamelessly employing epistemically dubious methods in forming beliefs on the other. It is easy to see that Ichikawa's account inherits this normative problem.[24] Ichikawa's view will deliver a uniform justification diagnosis for all these cases, since all these folks are in an intrinsic state that is consistent with them having knowledge. However, the former are intuitively epistemically better off than the latter.

Bird's picture does better on this front: according to him, there is a clear normative difference between blamelessness and justification; justified belief is not merely blameless, but praiseworthy (2007, 108). In aiming at knowledge, one can fail to reach one's aim while doing nothing wrong (blamelessly); that is, for instance, the case of someone who is brainwashed into believing a falsehood. In contrast, one can fail to believe knowledgeably while, at the same time, doing something right, that is, praiseworthy. This latter normative dimension, according to Bird, maps on to justified belief, and regards one's proper 'ordering' of one's mental life (2007, 108). Bird motivates his view as follows:

> [Some] failures can be laid at the door of the believer, because the source of failure is one or more of the believer's mental states, and some failures can be ascribed to mischance, in that the failure is due to some mentally extraneous factor. The role of the notion of justification is to mark the difference between these different sources of failure. (Bird 2007, 96)

According to Bird, then, the crucial role played by the concept of justification – that is, epistemic praiseworthiness – is to mark the difference between failure that is due to our environment and failure that is due to us.

---

[24] See also Hetherington (2002) for further worries affecting views that take epistemic justification to be a function of epistemic responsibility.

Now, here is the worry: Bird is a content externalist (as one should be). As such, what mental states one is in will not merely supervene on internal features of the subject. In this, Bird's justification is not solely dependent on matters internal to the believer: since being in a mental state or another depends on the environment, and since justification depends on being in a particular mental state, Bird's subjects will only host justified beliefs if they are in a friendly environment – that is, an environment in which they have the mental states required by would-be-knowledge. But then, it is not clear how his account of justification fits the motivations put forth in its support. After all, failure to be in the right mental state is not, as Bird puts it, something that can be fully 'laid at the door of the believer', any more than knowledge is. They both depend on the cooperation of the environment. The view remains silent on the normative significance of would-be-knowledge after all. *Mutatis mutandis*, more needs to be said in support of its prior plausibility.

2.3 Knowledge-First Virtue Epistemologies

Knowledge-first virtue epistemological accounts (e.g. Mirachi (2015), Kelp (2016, 2018, 2021), Lasonen-Aarnio (MS), Millar (2010), Schellenberg (2018)) unpack justified belief (broadly speaking) as belief formed via knowledge-generating abilities (or virtues, or capacities).

Millar and Schellenberg offer accounts of perceptual justification in the first instance. Millar's account is factive, so many of the things I said about JB=K views will apply to his account as well. Schellenberg (2018) develops what is strictly speaking a capacities-first rather than a knowledge-first view: on her view, justification is to be analysed in terms of knowledge, and knowledge is to be analysed in terms of capacities. Lasonen-Aarnio (MS) develops a knowledge-first dispositionalism about what she calls 'reasonable' belief.[25]

I will mainly focus here on Kelp and Mirrachi's views, which are the first and most paradigmatic of this way of thinking about justification.

On Kelp's view, successful belief is knowledge and justified belief is competent belief. In turn, a belief that p is competent insofar as it is formed via the exercise an ability to know propositions in a particular range R and relative to conditions C such that p $\in$ R.

---

[25] Paul Silva (2017) proposes a view that, depending on how it gets spelled out, could also qualify as a virtue epistemology. On this view, S has a justified belief iff S's belief is produced by an exercise of S's knowledge of how to gain propositional knowledge, and (ii) S is not justified in thinking she is not in a position to acquire propositional knowledge in her current circumstances. If one unpacks knowledge how along anti-intellectualist lines (e.g. Carter & Pritchard 2008), the view is a skill-based view, and thereby a virtue epistemology. If one prefers intellectualism, the account becomes implausibly overly intellectualized: justified believers require a bunch of propositional knowledge about ways of gaining propositional knowledge.

According to Miracchi, knowledge itself is an exercise of a competence to know, as is mere justification. The important difference is that, while knowledge manifests the relevant competence, mere justification is a degenerate exercise of a competence to know; some of the manifestation conditions – that is, whatever operations of subpersonal cognitive mechanisms and external conditions together constitute a particular case of knowing that p in the way characteristic of the competence – are absent.

These views too are normatively pluralist views in that they take the goal and norm of belief to come apart. In this, they allow for justified false belief, and justification in Gettier cases. Furthermore, in virtue of the richness of performance normativity, these views have the resources to offer an independent motivation for an externalist dimension to justification, which differentiates it from mere blamelessness.

On Kelp's account, for instance, while successful belief is knowledgeable belief, justified false believers, deceived victims, and Gettiered agents are justified in their beliefs because they are formed via the relevant competences. Finally, benighted cognizers are merely blameless cognizers. Miracchi's account (Forthcoming) goes one step further, proposing more normative dimensions: according to her, first, there is epistemic justification – an exercise of a competence to know (present e.g. in Gettier cases); second, there is the internalist counterpart of justification, epistemic rationality – consisting in properly valuing knowledge as the aim of one's belief (displayed by deceived victims) – and third, there is blameless belief.

The worry that arises for both Kelp and Miracchi is that the views threaten to be too agent-centric to account for cases of justification-affecting update failure. Here is why: on virtue theories, agential abilities (or capacities, or competencies) take explanatory priority and ground the epistemic normativity of belief. Traditionally, thus, virtue epistemologies unpack propositional justification in terms of doxastic justification (Turri 2010). However, a view like this will struggle to explain what goes wrong in cases of evidence resistance (Simion 2024c,d), that is, cases in which intuitively propositional justification is present and the agent does not form form/update accordingly due to lack of virtue/ability/competence. For instance, since sexists, racists, and wishful thinkers are, by definition, people who lack the dispositions to form true or knowledgeable beliefs on the relevant issues, we get the counterintuitive result that these subjects lack any propositional justification and thus are not doing anything wrong, epistemically, in not forming the corresponding beliefs.

Here is one move available to the virtue theorist: dispositions can fail to manifest themselves when 'masked'. When in a room filled with pillows, a vase is still fragile, although its disposition to break cannot manifest itself. Similarly, virtue theorists could argue, biased cognizers have the relevant epistemic abilities, but they are 'masked' by the presence of bias, wishful thinking, and so on.

The problem with this reply, however, is that factors that 'mask' dispositions are commonly believed to be environmental factors (Choi & Fara 2018) – for example, the room full of pillows – rather than factors somehow 'internal' to the item in question, such as biases and motivated reasonings; indeed, when the problem lies within the object itself – say that we inject all the pores of the vase with glue, for instance – the more plausible diagnosis is loss of disposition – no fragility – rather than masked disposition.

Why not hold that in some cases dispositions can be masked by internal factors, even though they are typically masked by environmental factors? The worry for this reply is one of ad hoc-ness: sometimes, dispositions are masked. Some other times, they are lost. We need a principled distinction between the former and the latter. The orthodox way to get at this distinction is to point out that masks safeguard against the manifestation of a disposition without threatening the disposition itself: for example, intuitively, the pillows don't remove the fragility of the vase, they merely prevent it from manifesting. However, there is no sense in which, for example, sexist cognizers are intuitively disposed to believe women.[26]

2.4 Knowledge-First Functionalism

In previous work (Simion 2019, 2024d), I have defended a knowledge-first account of justification which I have dubbed *Knowledge-First Functionalism*. Here is the view:

Knowledge-First Functionalism (KFF): A belief is *prima facie* justified if and only if it is generated by a properly functioning cognitive capacity that has the epistemic etiological function of generating knowledge.

It is easy to see that KFF follows straightforwardly from the etiological functionalist picture defended earlier, together with the claims that generating knowledge is the epistemic function of inquiry, and that, in virtue of being a move in inquiry, belief formation aims at knowledge.

That being said, in what follows, I will also venture to offer an argument for KFF on mere a priori grounds. I will argue that generating knowledge is the

---

[26] See Kelp (2023) for an account of cases of knowledge resistance in terms of epistemic proficiencies and Miracchi (2019) for an account of permissible suspension that predicts that these are cases where respect for knowledge is not manifested.

function of our belief formation systems, and that, in virtue of this knowledge function, justification turns on knowledge.

Here is the argument, in brief: Our belief formation systems are representational systems. Since to generate non-knowledgeable beliefs is to fail to successfully represent, the function of our belief formation systems is generating knowledge. Functions generate functional norms: functional items ought to work in ways that are, in normal conditions, conducive to function fulfilment. Since knowledge generating is the main representational function of our belief formation systems, my belief formation systems (representationally) ought to work in a manner that is, in normal conditions, conducive to generating knowledge. Belief formation systems that fail to do so are malfunctioning. The next step is to recall that justification turns on norm fulfilment: for all *phi* and norms of a particular type T, *phi* is T-justified if and only if *phi* is T-permissible. If so, one's belief that p is epistemically justified if and only if it is epistemically permissibly formed. Finally, note that, very plausibly, representational norms are epistemic norms. If all this is so – that is, if representational norms governing our belief formation turn on knowledge, and epistemic justification turns on representational norm fulfilment – it follows that epistemic justification turns on knowledge: beliefs are epistemically justified iff formed in a manner that is, in normal conditions, conducive to generating knowledge.

Here is the argument unpacked:[27]

(1) Representational systems have representational main functions.
(2) The representational function of a system is to successfully represent.
(3) If a subject S has a belief formation system, then it is a representational system.
(4) If S has a belief formation system, then its representational main function is to successfully represent (from 1 to 3).
(5) Belief formation systems successfully represent if and only if they generate knowledge.
(6) If S has a belief formation system, its representational main function is to generate knowledge (from 4 and 5).
(7) If x's function of type T is to *phi*, then x (T)-should work in a way that is conducive to *phi-ing* in normal conditions.
(8) If S has a belief formation system, then it (representationally) should work in a way that is conducive to generating knowledge in normal conditions. (from 6 and 7)
(9) Representational norms governing belief formation are epistemic norms.

---

[27] An early version of this argument can be found in my exchange with Aidan McGlynn for the *Contemporary Debates in Epistemology*, 3rd Edition (Simion 2024a,b).

(10) One's belief that p is epistemically justified iff it is epistemically permissibly formed.

(11) One's belief is epistemically justified iff it is formed in a way that is conducive to generating knowledge in normal conditions (from 8, 9, and 10).

I take (1) and (2) to not be in need of a lot of defence: some systems wear their main functions up their sleeves, in that their dubbing is function-driven. Plausibly, toasters have toasting main functions. Also plausibly, the toasting function of any system is to toast successfully. Washing machines have washing main functions, and the washing function of any system is to wash successfully. Representational systems have representational main functions, and their representational function is to successfully represent.

(3) assumes a view on the nature of our belief formation systems whereby their being representational systems is an essential feature of belief formation systems *qua* belief formation systems. I take this not to be in need of much defence either: after all, beliefs are representational devices, with mind to world direction of fit. That is not to say, of course, that one can know on a priori grounds that my eyes, for example, generate representations: surely, there could be a world populated by creatures that have the exact same mechanisms that we use for representing, only they use them, say, for digesting. It is an empirical question whether some given system is a belief formation system (Burge 2013). But if a psychological system *is* a belief formation system, its main function is to form representational devices (i.e. beliefs), hence to represent.

(4) follows from 1, 2, and 3.

(5) will likely be the source of much disagreement: representation, some will think, seems to be about truth, not knowledge. After all, what would be lost if we replaced 'successful representation' throughout in the argument with 'correct representation'? And if nothing would be lost, wouldn't a premise (5) thus reformulated be obviously false? Doesn't a representational system correctly represent something (e.g. the distance between two places) iff it is accurate? Two things in response: (1) first, one should worry about the claim that accuracy is enough for correct representation, since it does not suffice for representation *simpliciter*: Just because my three-year-old, while scribbling, happens to end up with something that is identical to the London Tube map, it doesn't follow that the drawing represents the London Tube. Representation is a relational property, accuracy is not. As such, the argument would go through even with 'represent' simpliciter. (2) For people who don't like the thought that representation is relational: literature has already pointed out that 'correct' is ambiguous between accurate and norm compliant (Schnurr 2017). The revamped argument earlier

rides on this ambiguity: *phi*-ing accurately is *phi*-ing correctly in one sense, but not the other.

Here are more reasons in support of (5). First, note that a belief that is not knowledgeable (false, or true by luck, or based on a hunch, or Gettierized) is intuitively defective *qua* belief. To see this, note that beliefs that fall short of knowledge in the various ways described earlier are intuitively criticizable (which, importantly, is not to say that the believers in question are: to the contrary, very plausibly, blamelessly non-knowledgeable believers are not criticizable). In turn, *ceteris absentibus* (i.e. unless there are other reasons for criticism present, that do not pertain to Xs goodness qua X), criticizability indicates lack of attributive goodness: *ceteris absentibus*, it cannot be that something X is criticizable although there is nothing attributively defective with X – that is, although X is good qua X.

As Williamson puts it, mere belief is botched knowledge (2000). Crucially, note also that knowledge is enough for non-defective belief: *ceteris absentibus* (e.g. in the absence of high practical stakes, or moral considerations against), there's nothing wrong – qua belief – with a knowledgeable belief that falls short of certainty, for instance. If all this is so, however, (5) follows: since it is plausible that a belief formation system is only successful if it generates attributively good beliefs – beliefs that are good qua beliefs – and since good beliefs are knowledgeable beliefs, it will follow that our belief formation systems are only successful if they generate knowledge.

To see the plausibility of (5) further, recall Putnam's famous ant case:

> THE ANT: An ant is crawling on a patch of sand. As it crawls, it traces a line in the sand. By pure chance the line that it traces curves and recrosses itself in such a way that it ends up looking like a recognizable caricature of Winston Churchill. Has the ant traced a picture of Winston Churchill, a picture that depicts Churchill? Most people would say, on a little reflection, that it has not. The ant, after all, has never seen Churchill, or even a picture of Churchill, and it had no intention of depicting Churchill. It simply traced a line [. . .] (Putnam 1982)

This case lends support to content externalism: the ant does not have the concept of Churchill, since she's never seen or heard of Churchill, and, as a result, the line it draws in the sand does not stand in the right relation to Churchill to count as representing Churchill.

Now, consider the following variation on this case:

> THE DANCER: Mary has been introduced to Winston Churchill and knows him well. Now, Mary is dancing salsa at a beach party and, unbeknownst to

> her, by pure chance, as she dances, she traces a line in the sand that ends up looking like a recognizable caricature of Winston Churchill.

Has Mary drawn a picture that successfully represents Winston Churchill? No: the line in the sand does not stand in the right relation to Churchill to count as representing Churchill. There is no difference between the ant's line in the sand and Mary's: Mary has the concept of Churchill, but the right relation for representation to be instantiated still fails to obtain: the causal chain, as it were, is interrupted on the segment from Mary's concept to the line in the sand: what explains the correlation is intervening luck (Pritchard 2005): luck that intervenes between Mary's concept of Churchill and the line she draws in the sand.[28] What this suggests is that representation, just like knowledge, is incompatible, in an important sense, with intervening luck. This, in turn, lends support to (5) earlier: systems generating luckily true beliefs are not successful representational systems, in virtue of not putting us in cognitive contact proper with the world. Forming lucky true beliefs does not amount to representing the world, just like Mary's dancing does not count as a representational process, no matter how many times she luckily ends up drawing Churchill-looking lines in the sand. What safeguards against intervening luck is knowledge: Representational belief formation systems are knowledgeable belief formation systems: they are systems that are only successful when they generate knowledge.

At this stage one might think something is still missing from the analogy: knowledge, one might think, but not proper representation, is also incompatible with environmental luck – the kind of luck present in Fake Barn-type cases.[29] In what follows, I will argue that considerations pertaining to the incompatibility of knowledge with epistemic risk give us strong reason to resist this push-back: I argue that knowledge is the norm of belief in virtue of the fact that justified true belief that falls short of knowledge is too risky to be a good token of its type.

There are three ways for some x to be too y. First, it can be that x is too y for a particular purpose present at a particular context. Second, when several purposes are salient at the context, something x can be too y all-present-purposes-considered, while, at the same time, not too y for some of them. Last

---

[28] Would intervening luck still be a problem if we retold the story such that Mary intends to draw Churchill? I think it would. Consider the following variation of the case: say that Mary intends to draw Churchill in the sand as she dances, but, having had too many cocktails, her dance moves track a perfect portrait of Theresa May. However, luckily for her, her dance partner, who has never even heard of Churchill, is also intoxicated, with the result that they both end up stumbling in funny ways – and, as a result, drawing a picture that looks exactly like Churchill in the sand. The intuition, I submit, doesn't change in this version of the case.

[29] Many thanks to Aidan McGlynn (in 2024a, 2024b, and conversation) for pressing me on this.

but not least, some *x* can be too *y simpliciter,* that is, too y to be a token of its type (as in Geach 1956)).

With this in mind, consider:

Fake Barns (adapted from Goldman 1976). Henry is driving in the countryside, looking at objects in fields. He sees what looks exactly like a barn. Accordingly, he believes that there is a barn in front of him. Now, that is indeed the case. But what he does not realize is that this county is populated with many fake barns – mere barn facades that look exactly like real barns when viewed from the road.

First, I submit that there is a strong intuition that Henry's belief is too risky. To see this, note that, if we were to find out that Henry, unbeknownst to him, is visiting Fake Barn County, we would be inclined to warn him: 'If you see something that looks like a barn, don't believe it, it's likely just a façade!' Given the description of the case, plausibly, the intuitive appropriateness of this instance of warning is sourced in the belief at issue being too risky. Note, also, that an even more explicit warning along the lines of 'Don't trust you're seeing barns, you run a high risk of being wrong!' also seems perfectly appropriate.

Second, the intuition that Henry's belief is too risky is vindicated by the main accounts of risk in the literature: on a probabilistic view (Boholm et al. 2016), because the probability of getting it wrong is very high; on a modal view (Pritchard 2014), because the world at which Henry gets things wrong is too close.

Third, note that the 'too risky' at stake in *Fake Barns* is of the third variety identified earlier: too risky *simpliciter.* After all, no particular purpose is present at the context; the case is not one where Henry is about to employ his belief that there is a barn in front of him for some aim or another, act on the relevant belief, base his decisions on it, tell anybody about this, and so on.

If that is the case, though, that is, if what is at stake is too risky *simpliciter,* then, it will regard attributive goodness; Henry's belief will be too risky to be a good token of its type, that is, too risky to be a good belief.

Note also that, were Henry to know that there is a barn in front of him – that is, were he not to be in Fake Barns County – his belief would not be too risky to be a good token of its type anymore.

If that is the case, on given that belief complies with the (evaluative) norm of belief only if it is a good belief, it follows that one's belief complies with the norm of belief only if knowledgeable. Also, we have one more argument that successful representation is incompatible with environmental luck: since successful representation implies attributively good belief, and belief in Fake Barn cases is too risky to be attributively good, it follows that Fake Barns cases are not cases of successful representation. Successful representation, then, just like knowledge, is strongly incompatible with both intervening and environmental luck.

I have argued that generating knowledge is the function of our belief formation systems (6). Further, I take (7) to be in no need of defence; functions are widely taken to generate corresponding norms.

(8) follows from (6) and (7), and (9) is eminently plausible. (10) is the incarnation for epistemic normativity of belief of the widely accepted deontic thesis for justification: justified *phi*-ing is permissible *phi*-ing. Finally, (11) follows from (8), (9), and (10): since belief's representational norms turn on knowledge, and since belief's epistemic justification turns on representational norms, the epistemic justification of belief turns on knowledge.

The previous argument vindicates KFF on a priori grounds. The etiological functionalist picture delivers it on plausible empirical grounds, having to do with the evolutionary success of our cognitive traits. In this, KFF scores exceptionally well on prior plausibility.

KFF also does well on extensional adequacy. On KFF, epistemic justification supervenes on the proper performance of cognitive capacities that have generating knowledge as their epistemic function. But proper functioning need not imply function fulfilment; our cognitive processes can function properly, but still fail to produce knowledgeable beliefs, due to unfriendly environmental conditions. In virtue of its normative richness, KFF can accommodate the intuition of justification for Gettierized, deceived victims, and conscientious false believers; these folks employ properly functioning cognitive processes that have the function of generating knowledge. In contrast, mere blameless believers employing dubious methods of belief formation – albeit, through no fault of their own – are not justified believers.

Second, consider Norman the Clairvoyant (Bonjour 1980): whenever the President is in New York, Norman forms a true belief that the President is in New York via his (unbeknownst to him) reliable clairvoyant capacities. Norman is a notable problem for reliabilism's sufficiency claim, since intuitively he is not justified to believe that the President is in New York. His belief also comes out as unjustified on KFF, in virtue of Norman not employing a process with the function of generating knowledge: clairvoyance does not have the relevant function, since it does not have a knowledge-generating history, and thus does not meet E-Function. At the same time, since KFF is based on a short-history etiological functionalist framework, it nicely delivers on the intuition that Swampman (Sosa 1993) can have justified beliefs as soon as he acquires the relevant concepts.

Last but not least: KFF fits snugly with recent work suggesting that cannot we justifiably (Kelp 2017) or rationally (Douven 2006, 2009) believe lottery propositions. KFF predicts as much: beliefs based on mere statistical data are not generated via knowledge-producing processes, since they cannot be knowledgeable.

Conclusion

Generating knowledge is the function of our belief forming cognitive capacities. In turn, justified belief turns on their proper functioning. This explains why justification turns on knowledge. This also helps explain why there can be justified false beliefs and Gettierized beliefs: justification maps on to the proper functioning of our knowledge-generating cognitive capacities, and proper function survives unfriendly environmental conditions.

3 Reasons, Evidence, and Defeat

Introduction

This section integrates the knowledge-first functionalist picture of justified belief with a unified account of reasons, evidence, and defeat. On this view, reasons are norm compliance indicators. In turn, pieces of evidence and defeat are epistemic reasons for and against believing. Since good belief – belief that complies with the evaluative norm for belief – is knowledgeable belief, evidence and defeat consist of knowledge and, respectively, ignorance indicators: facts that one is in a position to know and that, in normal conditions, either increase or decrease one's distance to knowledge.

3.1 Reasons For and Against

Normative reasons – be they for belief or action – explain why you ought to/are permitted to *phi* (believe, act, etc.). Motivating reasons explain why you *phi* in a normatively loaded way: in *phi*-ing, you *treat* them as normative, which is why you *phi*. They are putative normative reasons: In the good case, they actually are normative. In the bad case, they are not.[30]

Reasons are facts. They can, however, be facts about the world around us, or mere facts about a subject's psychology. My having a perception as of a table in front of me is a psychological fact; it (*pro tanto, prima facie*) supports the belief that there is a table in front of me. So does the fact that there is a table in plain view in front of me. My hearing you say that the Arctic Monkeys are playing

---

[30] Importantly, 'treating' is not a cognitively sophisticated affair: I can treat my cat as a friend without being aware that I do.

supports my going to the concert. So does the fact that the Arctic Monkeys are playing.

According to the view I prefer, normative reasons for are indicators of norm compliance. Here is the view:

Reasons For as Indicators of Norm Compliance: A fact F is a (*pro tanto, prima facie*[31]) reason of type T to *phi* iff it (*pro tanto, prima facie*) indicates that *phi*-ing conforms to the T-evaluative norm for *phi*-ing.

Conversely, normative reasons against are indicators of norm violation:

Reasons Against as Indicators of Norm Violation: A fact F is a (*pro tanto, prima facie*) reason of type T against *phi-ing* iff it (*pro tanto, prima facie*) indicates that *phi*-ing is in breach of the T-evaluative norm for *phi*-ing.

My hearing you say that the Arctic Monkeys are playing is a prudential reason for me to go to the concert. It is a (*pro tanto, prima facie*) indicator that my going to the concert is a prudentially good thing to do. Similarly, my having a perception as of a table in front of me is an epistemic reason for me to believe that there is a table in front of me. It is a (*pro tanto, prima facie*) indicator that my corresponding belief that there is a table in front of me is a good belief.

In order to get a more substantive account of a particular type (e.g. moral, prudential, epistemic) of reasons to *phi* (e.g. act, believe), we will need to take a stance on two things: what good *phi*-ing is, and how to unpack the relevant indicator relation. This Element's ambition is restricted to offering a substantive account of epistemic reasons for and against believing – that is, evidence and defeat. I have argued in the previous section that good belief is knowledgeable belief. What remains to be done, in order to understand reasons for and against believing, is to unpack the relevant indicator relation.[32]

---

[31] The account requires *pro tanto, prima facie* restrictions: that I have made a promise to a friend that requires me to go left is a (*pro tanto, prima facie*) reason to go left even when there is an emergency that requires me to go right because it *pro tanto prima facie* indicates that going left is morally good.

[32] Importantly, nothing that I will say about evidence and defeat (i.e. epistemic reasons to believe/ against believing) commits me to any particular way to unpack either reasons in general, or e.g. prudential/moral reasons for action: on my view, reasons are indicators of norm compliance, and evidence and defeat, in virtue of being a species of reasons (i.e. epistemic reasons), are indicators of epistemic norm compliance. In turn, these are unpacked probabilistically – but it need not follow that all reasons afford probabilistic unpacking (since species can have properties that the type does not have, and a particular species of a type T can have properties another species of T does not have: waltzing is a species of dancing; compatibly, it is governed by constitutive norms that do not govern mere dancing, nor tango dancing).

3.2 The Epistemic Support Relation

Evidence and defeat are reasons for and against believing, so they consist of facts. What kind of facts? In order to qualify as a subject S's evidence for p, facts need to describe a particular epistemic relation with regard to p, and a particular having relation with regard to S. What do these relations map on to?

Concerning the epistemic support relation: recall that I said that I take evidence and defeat to be epistemic reasons for/against believing, and that reasons are indicators of norm compliance/violation. I also said that, in order to put more flesh on the bones on the nature particular types of reasons, we need to unpack the indicator relation for that particular type of reasons.

Here is one straightforward way to do it (henceforth, 'the straightforward view'): we could think of the indicator relation as having to do with increasing probability. In turn, since good belief is knowledgeable belief, and since reasons for believing are indicators of evaluative norm compliance for belief – that is, knowledge indicators – we get a view whereby reasons for belief (or evidence) have to do increasing knowledge probability and reasons against belief (or defeaters) have to do with decreasing knowledge probability. (Gibbons 2013), (Dutant and Littlejohn 2021), and (Kelp 2023) propose a view that goes in this direction for defeat. On their account, broadly speaking, defeaters consist in evidence that one is not in a position to know. There are two main problems for accounts like these, however. The first is structural: these accounts are epistemically second order, in that defeaters are evidence that some epistemic status is missing. But for an agent to have this evidence, they need to be able to process the relevant content; many agents that can undergo defeat are not sophisticated enough to have the relevant contents, however.

The second problem parallels a wrong-kind-of-reasons problem: matters that are intuitively irrelevant to justification and defeat can be evidence for or against one being in a position to know. Here is a case adapted from Jonathan Jenkins-Ichikawa (from personal conversation): Say that your grandfather is not feeling well and you're searching for the thermometer to check whether he has a fever. Now, finding the thermometer is evidence (and a probability increaser) that you are in a position to know that your grandfather has a fever, and, indeed, evidence that you will come to know that he does. However, clearly, it does not affect the justification of your belief that he has a fever. Conversely, not finding the thermometer is evidence that you're not in a position to know that he does (and a knowledge probability decreaser), but it surely does not defeat whatever justification you might have had to believe that he does have a fever. Note, also, that this is a case of evidential irrelevance, not one of epistemic overdetermination (i.e. not one where I have redundant evidence). Epistemic overdetermination presupposes evidential relevance. But here, evidential relevance is absent.

The straightforward view doesn't work. Importantly, though, we don't need to go for the straightforward view when it comes to unpacking the indicator relation. Indicators of knowledge need not be knowledge probability increasers or decreasers.

When it comes to epistemic reasons for and against believing, my preferred way to unpack the indicator relation has to do with indicating an increase or decrease *in distance to* knowledge in normal conditions, via an increase or decrease in evidential probability. Here it goes:

In my view, evidence for p consists of facts that increase one's evidential probability that p is the case. The fact that I have a perception as though there is a table right in front of me is evidence for me that there is a table in front of me. It is a fact that increases the probability on my evidence that there is a table in front of me. Not just any psychological facts, then, will be evidence that there is a table in front of me: my having a perception as of a table will fit the bill in virtue of having the relevant indicator property. Perceptions are knowledge indicators; when I have a perception as of a table, my evidential probability of there being there's a table goes up. The fact that I wish that there was a table in front of me will not fit the bill, even if, unbeknownst to me, my table wishes are strongly correlated with the presence of tables: wishes are not knowledge indicators – they don't increase the probability on my evidence that there is a table in front of me. For the same reason, mere beliefs, as opposed to justified and knowledgeable beliefs, will not be evidence material; they lack the relevant indicator property.

Here is the view:

The Epistemic Support Relation: A fact (*pro tanto, prima facie*) epistemically supports p for S if and only if it increases the S's evidential probability that p (Simion 2023, 2024c,d, Williamson 2000).

Conversely on this account, defeaters will be ignorance indicators: they will be facts that lower S's evidential probability that p is the case.[33] Defeaters increase distance to knowledge in normal conditions: they decrease one's evidential probability – that is, the probability on one's total body of evidence – of *p* being the case.

---

[33] I have developed, defended, and presented my account of epistemic reasons, evidence, and defeat as knowledge/ignorance indicators starting back in 2018. Dutant and Littlejohn (2021) also call defeaters 'ignorance indicators', but, as we've already seen, their account is spelled out in very different terms, so any affinity is merely terminological.

Crucially, in my view, rebutting and undercutting defeaters share one and the same central epistemic normative property: they are evidential probability decreasers. What differs is the mechanism by which they achieve this effect: rebutters lower one's evidential probability for p by raising one's evidential probability for not-p. In contrast, undercutters reduce the degree of confirmation (Kotzen 2019) that a particular piece of evidence e confers on p – that is, the degree to which e probabilifies p on my evidence.

This unified treatment comes in contrast to literature that gives different treatment to first- and higher-order evidence, or rebutting and undercutting defeat. Most centrally for my purposes here, my unified account opposes a variety of scepticism about higher-order defeat for knowledge that has been introduced and made popular in knowledge-first epistemology by Maria Lasonen-Aarnio's work on the topic (e.g. 2014) and endorsed by Tim Williamson (Forthcoming).

I think mine is the right result: undercutters and rebutters afford a unified treatment, and we should, all else equal, prefer this unified treatment on grounds having to do with theoretical adequacy. Here are some further reasons to prefer my account: one's confidence in p should match the degree of confirmation that one's evidence offers to p – the degree to which one's evidence probabilifies p. Now, here is a case of higher-order evidence that increases the degree of confirmation of the first-order evidence: I believe p based on my neighbour's George's testimony. Mary tells me that George is the top expert in the world on the matter. Her testimony is evidence that q: 'George's testimony gives very high support to p'. If George's original testimony probabilifies p to x, Mary's testimony translates roughly as 'George's testimony probabilifies p to y & y>x (how high y is will depend on Mary's epistemic credentials). So now that Mary has spoken, I am in a position to know that, for example, r: I have a .8 credence that p based on George's testimony and the probability that p conditional on George's testimony is .9. Intuitively: I should revise to .9. Now consider an analogous case of undercutting defeat: I believe p (indeed, I know p) based on my neighbour's George's testimony. Mary tells me that George is a well-known liar on p-issues. Her testimony is evidence that q: 'George's testimony gives lower support to p'. George's original testimony probabilifies p to x; Mary's testimony, just like before, amounts to: 'George's testimony probabilifies p to y & y<x (it will depend on Mary's epistemic credentials how low y is). Just like before, I am in a position to know that r: I have a .8 credence that p based on George's testimony and the probability that p conditional on George's testimony is .4. Intuitively, I should revise to .4.

Similarly, say that my impeccably executed mathematical proof supports p, but, at the same time, I have evidence that my mathematical capacities may be diminished due to a drug I took. Initially, the proof evidentially probabilifies p to 1 for me. The evidence about the drug amounts to: 'The proof probabilifies p to y & y<x (it will depend on the strength of my evidence about the drug how low y is, let's say .5). I am now in a position to know that r: I have credence 1 that p based on the proof and the probability that p conditional on the proof is .5. Intuitively, I should revise to .5.

Defeat affords a unified treatment, and one should not be sceptical about knowledge defeat.

3.3 The Having Relation

In the previous section, I said that, in order to qualify as a subject S's evidence/defeaters for p, facts need to describe a particular epistemic relation with regard to p, and a particular having relation with regard to S. In line with Williamson 2000, I have defended a probabilistic account of the epistemic relation. The question that remains to be answered is the question of the nature of the having relation. When is a piece of evidence properly describable as had by a subject?

Famously, Tim Williamson thinks that one's evidence is one's knowledge (E=K). It is here where we part ways.

To see why, I would like to start by noting that the ways in which we think of evidence outside of and within philosophy come apart: in philosophy we disagree a lot about the nature of evidence, but one thing the vast majority of theorists have always assumed is that the having relation is somehow related to the limits of one's skull: one has evidence, on this received view, when one uptakes it 'in one's head' – be it via seemings, beliefs, knowings,[34] and so on. In contrast, outside of philosophy, the having relation has never been about the skull: just try to tell a judge that you had no evidence that the butler did it, even though he did it right in front of you, because you couldn't believe your eyes; see how that goes down.

I think the folk account is the correct one: the philosophical conception of the having relation – as having to do with some instantiation within the limits of one's skull – fails on both extensional grounds and prior plausibility (Simion 2023, 2024c,d). It will be instructive for our purposes here to see how this affects E=K.

Consider the following case:

Friendly Detective: Detective Dave is investigating a crime scene. Dave is extremely thorough, but, at the same time, a close friend of the butler. Dave finds conclusive evidence that the butler did it – the butler's gloves covered in

---

[34] Of course, knowledge is not limited to one's skull – but a knowledge view of evidence requires belief, so in this sense it requires evidence to be inside one's skull.

blood, his fingerprints on the murder weapon, a letter written by the butler confessing to the crime – but fails to form the corresponding beliefs: Dave just can't get himself to believe that his friend would do such a thing, so he fails to form the beliefs that the butler's gloves are covered in blood, his fingerprints on the murder weapon, and so on.

According to E=K, Dave's evidence is Dave's knowledge. However, Dave does not believe, and therefore does not know that the butler did it, nor that the butler's gloves are covered in blood, his fingerprints on the murder weapon, and so on, and thus, on this view, has no evidence that the butler did it. But if that's the case, it is mysterious why we should think there is anything epistemically criticizable about Dave's doxastic attitudes in this case.

One alternative way to account for what is going on in this case is to say that the Detective, although he doesn't have evidence of the butler's guilt, is blameworthy for not having it – which explains our intuition of impermissibility.[35] Had Dave not had bad epistemic dispositions, he would have had this evidence. One important problem with this move, however, is that it is both too weak and too strong. To see why it is too weak, consider the case of two detectives, Dave1 and Dave2, investigating a crime scene with the aim of determining whether the butler did it. Dave1 is just like our original Friendly Detective. In contrast, Dave2 is rather lazy and distracted: he shallowly looks around the crime scene a couple of times, fails to notice anything of importance, and concludes that there's no evidence to suggest that the butler did it. As a result, he suspends judgment. I submit that both Dave1 and Dave2 are rather rubbish detectives, and have bad epistemic dispositions. Compatibly, I submit, there is an important intuitive epistemic difference between Dave1 and Dave2: Dave, but not Dave2 has evidence in support of the hypothesis that the butler did it, and fails to form the relevant belief nevertheless.

What is needed is a principled way to identify the epistemic dispositions that matter. Note that Williamson's own dispositional account of blameworthiness (Forthcoming) will not do the trick: both detectives violate both the secondary norm of belief (because they do not have a disposition to believe knowledgeably) and the tertiary norm of belief (because they do not do what a knowledgeable believer would do).

To see why the view is also too strong, note that one need not have bad epistemic dispositions in order to fail, epistemically, in the way in which Dave does: it can be a one-off affair. Maybe Dave is an excellent epistemic agent in all other walks of life: it's only on this particular topic that he refuses to form a belief against all facts speaking in favour of it.

---

[35] In conversation, Tim Williamson expressed a preference for this option.

Can we do better? I think we can. Here is my preferred view (2023, 2024):

The Having Relation: S has a piece of evidence e/a defeater d if and only if S is in a position to know that e/d (Simion 2023, 2024c,d).

What is it for me to be in a position to know a fact?[36] Plausibly, a certain availability relation needs to be instantiated. On my view, availability has little to do with the limits of my skull. Evidence may consist of facts 'in the head' or facts in the world. Some facts – whether they are in the head or in the world, it does not matter – are available to me, they are, as it were, 'at hand' in my (internal or external) epistemic environment. Some – whether in the head (think of justified implicit beliefs, for instance) or in the world, it does not matter – are not thus available to me.

Here are, for starters, some paradigmatic cases that illustrate what I'm talking about: If there is a table right in front of me, but I'm not forming the corresponding belief, I have evidence that there is a table in front of me. If, unbeknownst to me, you put a new table in the other room, the fact that you put it is there is *not available* to me: it is not evidence *that I have*. Similarly, if I have some mental state that is so deeply buried in my psychology that I can't access it, it is not evidence that I have.

My notion of availability will track a 'can' for an average cognizer of the sort exemplified. Here is some theory about this: first, there are *qualitative* limitations on availability: we are cognitively limited creatures. There are of *types* information that we just cannot access, or process: the fact that there is a table in front of me is something that I can easily enough access. Your secret decision to put the table in the other room is not something I can easily access. There are also types of support relations that we cannot process: The fact that your car is in the driveway is evidence *for me* that you are home. But it's not evidence for my three-year-old son Max to believe that you are home. Max belongs to a variety of epistemic agents that are not sophisticated enough to process[37] the support

---

[36] Errol Lord spells out the having relation for reasons in terms of being in a position to know: on Lord's view, A fact is a reason r you possess to ϕ iff you are in a position to (i) know that r, and (ii) manifest knowledge about how to use r as a reason to ϕ, where to be in a position to manifest knowledge about how to use r as a reason to ϕ is to be disposed to ϕ whenever r is a reason to ϕ and you are in a position to know that r (2018, 121). It is this latter condition that worries me: to see why, think again about sexist cognizers: since sexism is a cognitive vice – that is, a disposition to disbelieve what women say – sexist cognizers will fail Lord's condition (ii): they will not be in a position to manifest knowledge about how to use the fact that a woman said that p as a reason to believe that p. Nevertheless, we don't want our view to predict that sexists don't have reasons to believe what women say.

[37] What is the relation between processing the support relation and knowledge indicators as probability enhancers? Is one supposed to be able to form probability beliefs in order to count as being able to process the support relation? The answer is 'no:' merely treating an indicator as such is enough; awareness of its being one is not needed, neither is awareness of what makes

relation into a belief that you are home. Evidence is not available to you if the kind of epistemic agent that you are cannot access or process the particular variety thereof at stake (henceforth also *Qualitative Availability*).

In this, crucially, the having relation and the epistemic support relation *are not independent from each other*: in order to have a piece of evidence, being attuned to the support relation is necessary: if, unbeknownst to me, whenever you wear a red dress there is rain in Spain, it does not follow that I have evidence that it is raining in Spain upon noticing that you are wearing a red dress.

There are also *quantitative* limitations on my information accessing and processing: the fact that there is a table somewhere towards the periphery of my visual field – in contrast with it being right in front of me, in plain view – is not something I can easily process: I lack the power to process everything in my visual field, it's just too much information (henceforth also *Quantitative Availability*).

The 'can' at stake here will be further restricted by features of the social and physical environment: we are supposed to read the newspaper on the table in front of us, but not the letter under the doormat. That's because we can't read everything, and our social environment and social roles are thus normatively constituted. I am supposed to look for the crocodiles in the lake but not in the fridge. That's because I can't look everywhere, and the laws of nature make it such that they're more likely to be in the lake (henceforth also *Environmental Availability*).

In sum: for a fact to be such that I am in a position to know it, it needs to be at hand for me in my epistemic environment: at hand qualitatively (it needs to be the *type* of thing a creature like me can access and process), quantitatively (it needs to remain within the *set of facts* a creature like me can access and process at one particular time), and environmentally (it needs to be easily *available* in my – internal or external – epistemic environment, that is, in my mind, or in my physical surroundings, or the kind of thing that my social situation makes normatively available).[38]

I take this availability relation to have to do with a fact being within the easy reach of my knowledge generating cognitive processes. A fact F being such that I am in a position to know it has to do with the capacity of my properly functioning knowledge generating processes to take up F:

Being in a Position to Know (BPK): S is in a position to know a fact F if S has a cognitive capacity with the function of generating knowledge that can

---

a fact into an indicator. 'Treating' is a lowbrow affair: I can treat my cat as a friend without believing that she is.

[38] See also Goldberg (2016, 2018).

(qualitatively, quantitatively, and environmentally) easily uptake F in cognizers of S's type.

A couple of things about this account: First, note that BPK is a sufficiency claim: it is not necessary that F is available to me in order for me to be in a position to know F: I can also come to know F via taking up other evidence for F.

Second, it is important to distinguish between being in a position to know and being in a position to *come* to know:[39] I am in a position to know that there is a computer in front of me; I am not in a position to know what is happening in the other room. I am, however, in a position to come to know it. Roughly, then, the distinction will, once more, have to do with epistemic availability: if all that needs to happen for me to come to know F is that my relevant cognitive processes take up F and process it accordingly, then I am in a position to know F. If more needs to be the case – I need to open my eyes, or turn around, or go to the other room, or give you a call – I am in a position to come to know F, but not in a position to know it.

Third, note that BPK is a restricted ought-implies-can: agent obligations imply capacities in the type of cognizer that she is. In turn, 'S's type' will be individuated by things like cognitive architecture, and physical and social normative situatedness. In this, the account will predict biased cognizers are in breach of their epistemic obligations: they may be unable to, for example, believe women because of bias, but cognizers with their cognitive capacities can form beliefs based on women's testimony, therefore they should. In virtue of building social situatedness into the type of cognizer at stake, the account will also predict that cases of breach of obligations to inquire – in which S's social role makes it such that S should have known that p is the case (e.g. Goldberg 2018) – are cases in which justification is defeated. To be sure, the view will be somewhat affected by a generality problem when it comes to individuating the type of cognizer at stake for the normative evaluation: that being said, I am not worried much about this: first, because most externalisms follow suit in this regard. Second, because I think we have a good intuitive grasp on this.

3.4 Justification, Evidence, and Defeat

With both the epistemic relation and the having relation at hand, we have full accounts of evidence and defeat:

---

[39] See Kearl and Willard-Kyle Forthcoming for critical discussion. Many thanks to Ernie Sosa and Matt McGrath for pressing me on this.

Evidence as Knowledge Indicators: a fact *e* is evidence for one for a proposition *p* just in case one is in a position to know *e*, and one's evidential probability that *p* is the case conditional on *e* is higher than one's unconditional evidential probability that *p* is the case.

Conversely, defeaters are indicators of ignorance: they are facts that one is in a position to know, and that lower one's evidential probability that p is the case:

Defeaters as Ignorance Indicators: a fact d is a defeater for S's evidence e for p iff S is in a position to know d and S's evidential probability that p conditional on e&d is lower than S's evidential probability that p conditional on e.

A few clarifications about how things hang together so far: First, what is the relation between reasons in general, and evidence and defeat? On my view, reasons are indicators of norm compliance, and evidence and defeat, in virtue of being a species of reasons (to wit, a species of epistemic reasons, that is, epistemic reasons for and against believing), are indicators of epistemic norm compliance – that is, knowledge indicators. In turn, these are unpacked probabilistically. Compatibly, it need not follow that all reasons (nor all epistemic reasons) afford probabilistic unpacking (since species can have properties that the type does not have, and that other species do not have: waltzing is a species of dancing, but is constituted by very many norms that do not govern dancing in general, not tango dancing). I am thus not defending a probabilistic view of reasons in general, nor of epistemic reasons in general, but rather only a probabilistic view of epistemic reasons for/against believing – that is, evidence and defeat. The latter does not commit me to the former: it is compatible with my view that, for example, prudential reasons for action will indicate norm compliance via different mechanisms (depending on how the indicator relation is spelled out).

Second, what is the relation between justified belief, evidence, and defeat? Some evidence and defeaters I take up with my belief formation machinery, while some I fail to take up, although I should. What grounds this 'should', in my view, is proper epistemic functioning.[40] Because they are knowledge indicators, pieces of evidence are justification makers: they are the proper inputs to our processes of belief formation, and when we have enough thereof, and the processes in question are properly functioning in all other ways, the resulting belief is epistemically justified. In turn, when our belief formation processes either fail to take up knowledge/ignorance indicators that they could have easily taken up, or they take them up but fail to update accordingly, they are malfunctioning. A subject S's belief formation capacity C will be malfunctioning

---

[40] See e.g. Burge (2003, 2020), Graham (2012), Millikan (1984), Simion (2021).

epistemically, for instance, if S has sufficient evidence supporting p that is available to be taken up via C and C fails to output a belief that p.

Note, however, that, since I can only take up a limited number of facts with my knowledge-generating processes, I will most often be in a situation where I can only take up a subset of the facts lying in plain view. The question that arises is: which is the subset that takes normative primacy, and thereby delivers my body of evidence/defeat, and affects the justification of my beliefs? Availability rankings will deliver the relevant set, on my view: the most easily available subset of facts that I can take up delivers the set of evidence I have: in the case of visual perception, for instance, facts located right in front of me, in the centre of my visual field, which are the brightest, and clearest, and so on – in general facts that are most easily available to the cognitive processes of a creature like me.[41]

Here are a few theoretical virtues of this account; first, it is naturalistically friendly, in that it situates the epistemic normativity of evidence and defeat within an etiological functionalist picture of normativity: epistemic oughts to update based on evidence and defeat have to do with the proper function of our cognitive processes, just like biological oughts to take up oxygen have to do with the proper function of our respiratory systems.

Second, in line with intuition, it predicts that there is evidence for the Gettierized victim that there is a sheep in the field: the fact that they have a perception as of a sheep is a fact that they are in a position to know and that raises their evidential probability that there is a sheep in the field. Also, there is evidence for the (recently envatted) Brain in the Vat for p: 'There is a tree in front of me' when she has a perceptual experience as of a tree, since that is a fact that she is in a position to know and that raises their evidential probability that there is a tree in front of her.

There is no evidence for Norman the clairvoyant that the President is in New York: clairvoyant experiences are non-evidential probability raisers when one is ignorant of the reliability of clairvoyance.

The account deals exceptionally well with cases of evidence and defeat resistance (Simion 2023, 2024c,d). It will be useful to compare my account to E = K once more on this front. In *Knowledge and Its Limits*, Williamson

---

[41] Tim Williamson (p.c.) worries that there will be cases where too many facts (too many for my quantitative limitations) will have the same availability ranking. I suspect the worry can mostly be alleviated by our relation to space, time, complexity, brightness, and so on. Maybe the easiest case to imagine along these lines is the case of very simple arithmetical truths. However, these are cases pertaining to the normativity of attention and inquiry: which of the equally accessible such truths should I focus on? Plausibly, other normative constraints will have to decide the issue. After we have the answer to this question, the most easily available set will constitute my evidence. Thanks also to Matt McGrath for many discussions on this topic.

considers an account of evidence in terms of being in a position to know, and he dismisses it based on the following rationale:

> [...] suppose that I am in a position to know any one of the propositions $p_1, \ldots, p_n$ without being in a position to know all of them; there is a limit to how many things I can attend to at once. Suppose that in fact I know p_1 and do not know $p_2, \ldots, p_n$. According to E = K, my evidence includes only p_1; according to the critic, it includes $p_1, \ldots, p_n$. Let q be a proposition which is highly probable given $p_1, \ldots, p_n$ together, but highly improbable given any proper subset of them; the rest of my evidence is irrelevant to q. According to E = K, q is highly improbable on my evidence. According to the critic, q is highly probable on my evidence. E = K gives the more plausible verdict, because the high probability of q depends on an evidence set to which as a whole I have no access. (Williamson 2000, 189)

Two things about this: first, note that, in virtue of the quantitative limitations that my account imposes on being in a position to know, the view does not suffer from the problem Williamson points to here. Indeed, given that there is a limit to how many things I can attend to at once, it is only the most available subset that I can attend to that is part of my body of evidence. Thus, on my view, if a fact is not part of the set of facts that I can uptake, given my limitations, then that fact is not one that I am in a position to know.

Even more importantly, I submit that once we put flesh on the bones of Williamson's case, my view, and not E = K, gives the intuitively right prediction. Here it goes:

> FRIENDLY DETECTIVE 2: It's highly probable that John killed the victim given that (p_1) John is a butler, (p_2) John is a very nice guy with an impeccable record, and (p_3) the only butler who's a very nice guy with an impeccable record was seen stabbing the victim. Friendly Detective is told p_1, p_2, and p_3 but can't get himself to believe p_3 because of wishful thinking, and he believes John didn't do it based on p_1 and p_2.

FRIENDLY DETECTIVE 2 is an instance of Williamson's case. However, it is E=K that delivers the counterintuitive result here: according to E = K, the detective is justified to believe John didn't do it. My view disagrees, and it scores on extensional adequacy.

Conclusion

I have defended a view on which normative reasons for are indicators of norm compliance, and normative reasons against are indicators of norm violation. Correspondingly, I have argued, epistemic reasons for and against believing – that is, evidence and defeaters – are indicators of knowledge, respectively ignorance: they affect my distance to knowledge in normal conditions, by increasing or decreasing my evidential probability that p is the case.

4 Action and Assertion

Introduction

Several philosophers defend a knowledge norm for action: one's action is permissible, the thought goes, if and only if it is based on knowledge. Many also find it plausible that assertion, in virtue of being a species of action, is governed by a knowledge norm. This section breaks ranks with this commonality claim: while assertion is epistemically permissible just in case it is knowledgeable, there is no epistemic norm for action; or so I argue.

4.1 The Normativity of Action

One central debate in recent literature on epistemic normativity concerns the epistemic norm for action. Several people endorse a knowledge norm: they think that one's action is permissible just in case it is based on knowledge (e.g. Hawthorne and Stanley (2008)). The most notable competing account claims that the epistemic support required for acting on p varies with context (e.g. Brown 2008). One such view comes from the Bayesian camp: on this view, one's action is permissible insofar as it maximizes expected utility (e.g. Douven (2008)).[42] Knowledge that p is not necessary for permissible action based on p: a (rational) credence that p will do the work just fine (in combination with the respective utilities). Furthermore, there will be cases in which knowledge that p will also not be sufficient for acting on p: more epistemic support may be needed (given the utilities involved).

The knowledge norm is thought to be strongly supported by the intuitive impermissibility of throwing out one's lottery ticket on mere probabilistic grounds (for the necessity direction), and the intuitive criticizability of cases of inaction in the presence of knowledge: 'You knew he was skipping school, you should have done something about it!' (for sufficiency).

The main problem for the necessity direction of the knowledge norm comes from cases like the following: say that you don't know that it will rain today, nor that it is likely to rain (nor do you have any other relevant piece of knowledge, for example, that you don't know whether it will rain or not). Indeed, you have no idea what the chances of rain might be. Nevertheless, it seems permissible to take your umbrella: after all, the costs involved in carrying it around are

---

[42] For an overview of the debate, see Benton (2014).

minimal, and the disutility involved in getting wet is high. Bayesian norms have an easy time accommodating this intuition; the knowledge norm struggles.

The main problem for the sufficiency direction of the knowledge norm comes from high-stakes cases (Brown 2018): a surgeon might know that it is the left kidney that needs to be removed (from testimony, examining the patient, test results, etc.), but it seems perfectly rational (and indeed, it is professionally required) for them to check again before cutting into the patient.

This section argues that the debate is afflicted by a category mistake: strictly speaking, there is no such thing as an epistemic norm for action.

Let us, on a first approximation, formulate the norm we are talking about as follows:

The X Norm For Action (XNA): One is in a good enough epistemic position to act on p only if p has X.

Now, as we have seen, there is no consensus in the literature as to what property X is supposed to stand for (whether it is knowledge, the required rational credence given the utilities, etc.). Many people, though, take it that XNA is a distinctively epistemic norm; according to Matt Benton, for instance, '[...] when one faces a decision over whether to act that depends on the truth of some proposition, then acting without knowing that proposition can seem epistemically suspect and deserving of criticism' (Benton 2014). Similarly, Martin Montminy argues that '[i]t is epistemically appropriate to act on the belief that p if and only if that belief counts as knowledge' (2012, p. 63). Also in support of a knowledge norm for action, John Hawthorne wonders whether winners of a bet with extremely good odds are 'epistemically laudable for taking the bet' (John Hawthorne 2004, p. 175).

Foes of the knowledge norm also agree about the genuine epistemic nature of the requirement on action at stake. According to Mikkel Gerken, for instance, '[...] if the profiles of epistemic assessment for action and assertion are relevantly similar, it is *prima facie* evidence for the assumption that the relevant epistemic norms are also relevantly similar' (Gerken 2014, 726).

Furthermore, people involved in the debate take XNA to be an epistemic norm in virtue of the fact that it concerns how good one's epistemic position needs to be vis-à-vis *p* in order to make acting on *p* permissible. Thus, both sides of the debate seem to stand behind a principle I call Content Individuation:

Content Individuation (CI). A norm, N, is a distinctively epistemic norm if and only if it regulates the epistemic properties required for proper *phi*-ing.

I have argued extensively that CI is false in previous work (e.g. Simion 2018c, 2021). In a nutshell, the problem with CI is that it's not a proper way to individuate norms of any type. When permissible action requires more or less of a gradable property G, all norms N regulating that particular type of action can fix the threshold for N-proper performance lower or higher on the G spectrum: it can be prudentially or morally appropriate to drive faster or slower, to have a better or a worse grade average, to speak louder or more quietly, and so on. Just because a norm is regulating the appropriate speed, it need not follow that it is a traffic norm; just because a norm regulates the appropriate tone of one's voice, it need not follow it is a norm of etiquette.

Now, action is certainly governed by many norms – prudential and moral norms are the most obvious candidates – and justification is a gradable property. Therefore, unless we are given reasons to believe epistemic normativity is somehow special in this respect, we should expect norms regulating the degree of epistemic justification required for proper action to make no exception; we should expect that just because a norm N affects the amount of justification needed for proper action, it need not follow that N is an epistemic norm. Just because a norm regulates the amount of epistemic support needed for proper action, it need not follow that it regulates the amount of epistemic support needed for *epistemically* proper action.

Given that CI is false, however, there is no reason to think that XNA is an epistemic norm for action: good enough epistemic position need not mean epistemically good enough, that is, it need not mean good enough by the epistemic norm. One can be in a prudentially good enough epistemic position (i.e. have enough epistemic support for prudentially good action)), a morally good enough epistemic position (e.g. have enough epistemic support for morally good action), and so on.

Note, also, that it is plausible that non-philosophers and philosophers alike will have a hard time distinguishing between different intuitions of propriety – which makes relying on 'natural' dialogues about how much epistemic support is needed for proper action hard: what we can ascertain via this methodology is an intuition of all-things-considered propriety/impropriety. It is a further and technical question what type propriety is overriding at the context.

Section 1 identified a straightforward way to go about distinguishing epistemic norms proper from mere norms with epistemic content, via the functions served. As such, on this account, XNA is going to express a genuinely epistemic norm just in case the relevant action promotes some epistemic function. In turn, prudential norms will be borne out by prudential functions, while epistemic norms will be concerned with reliably fulfilling epistemic functions in normal conditions.

Notice that most actions do not serve epistemic functions; my eating breakfast, running in the park, brushing my teeth, buying chocolate, helping my old neighbour cross the street are cases in point. Most of them have prudential functions, some of them have moral functions, maybe a few have aesthetic functions. In the absence of any characteristic epistemic function, though, there is little reason to think that these actions will be governed by an epistemic norm.

Consider, in contrast, asserting, perceiving, reporting, judging, learning, reading, and so on. These actions all have epistemic functions: generating knowledge, acquiring it, sharing it, and so on. As such, it makes sense for them to be governed by epistemic norms.

The general type 'action' does not serve an epistemic function and is thereby not governed by an epistemic norm. Note, however, that nothing I have said so far concerns the epistemic norm for practical reasoning; that is because, while action doesn't serve any epistemic function, it may still be that practical reasoning does. Indeed, the next section will argue that practical reasoning has the epistemic function of generating knowledge of what one ought to do.

One question that arises at this stage is: couldn't defenders of one account or another of the epistemic norm for action merely retreat in a discussion about practical reasoning? Furthermore, wasn't talk of 'the epistemic norm for action' mere loose talk to begin with – in that, what the debate has always *really* been about is the epistemic norm for practical reasoning?

Three things about this; first, we have seen already that several participants in the debate are very explicit that what they are talking about is action. Second, I would see a retreat to discussing practical reasoning but not action as a great success of my work. Third, and most importantly, though, the retreat would not be a 'mere retreat' at all, but it would rather require a fairly substantial revision of methodology. Here is why: most cases put forth in defence or one account or another of the epistemic norm for action appeal to intuitions about propriety of acting in a particular situation. If this section is right, however, the intuitive propriety of a particular action says little about the *epistemic* propriety of practical reasoning: the *prudential* propriety of an instance of practical reasoning may bear some relation the prudential propriety of the generated piece of action; importantly, though, epistemic propriety will not. Indeed, for instance, if my account is correct, the central cases that Bayesians and knowledge norm champions have pressed against each other in this literature are dialectically impotent: we can have Bayesianism for the prudential propriety of action, and a knowledge norm for practical reasoning. On a picture like this, it is (prudentially) permissible to take the umbrella even though you don't know it's going to rain, nor do you know that it's likely to rain (because, say, you only have a .6 credence that it's likely to rain, rather than a full belief). After all, it's not very costly to take the umbrella, and the disutility involved in being soaking wet is high. It may well be that it is also prudentially permissible to reason from 'It's likely going to rain' to the conclusion that you should take the umbrella, even though you don't know that it's likely going to rain. It's a prudentially useful inference to go through, since it's likely to generate the corresponding action. At the same time, it will be *epistemically* impermissible to reason from 'It's going to rain' to the conclusion that you should take the umbrella, given that you don't know that it's going to rain.

Action in general is not governed by an epistemic norm. One interesting by-product of this result concerns the assertion-action commonality assumption:[43] the previous results undermine commonality, together with the motivation behind it. Assertion is not governed by an epistemic norm in virtue of its being a species of action, but due to its characteristic epistemic function. The next sections develop this idea further.

4.2 Assertion Functionalism

One (epistemically) may: assert p if and only if one knows that p. This very popular view has become known in the literature as the Knowledge Norm of Assertion (KNA). The locus classicus for the defence of KNA is (Williamson 2000). The view has quite a lot going for it in terms of extensional adequacy: linguistic data concerning the paradoxical nature of assertions of the form 'p but I don't know that p', the fact that assertions can be challenged by the question, 'How do you know that p?', and the intuitive impropriety of asserting lottery propositions suggest that knowledge is necessary for epistemically permissible assertion; criticisms of the form 'You should have said something, you knew that p!' suggest that knowledge is also (epistemically) enough (Simion 2016). Compatibly, however, an extensionally adequate view is not yet an explanatorily adequate view, nor yet a view that enjoys prior plausibility. More work is needed.

Williamson (2000) thinks the knowledge norm is constitutive of assertion in the same way as rules of games and languages are constitutive. I have argued against this model in previous work (e.g. Kelp & Simion 2021). For our purposes here too, this model will not give us much in the way of explanatory richness: after all, constitutive norms of games and languages come about rather randomly. If we are to take the analogy seriously, then, we may conclude that the norm of assertion just happens to be knowledge and could have easily been something else. I find this unsatisfactory. Again, more work is needed to motivate a knowledge norm and explain the source of its normative strength.

Now, recall that the functionalist picture constitutes itself in a straightforward norm-identification machinery; first, we identify the function served by the trait/

---

[43] See Brown (2012) for discussion.

artefact/action in question. Once the function is identified, the question we need to ask ourselves is: how does the trait/artefact/action fulfil its function in normal conditions? This will give us proper functioning. As such, the answer to the function question delivers the content of the norm we are after, together with an explanation of why the norm is in force (because it delivers function fulfilment in normal conditions). Furthermore, on this picture, we also get an easy way to identify the type of norm at stake: norms will be typed by the corresponding functions, which, in turn, are typed by the produced benefit.

What is assertion's epistemic function? Although not essentially – I can make assertions in a diary, which are usually not intended to affect any audience in any way, and I can make assertions about the weather just for social bonding purposes –, characteristically, assertions will aim at generating testimonial knowledge in the audience. Plausibly, this is the main epistemic function of assertion (see, e.g., Kelp (2018), Kelp & Simion (2021), Simion (2021), Reynolds (2002)). Due to our physical and cognitive limitations, a lot of the knowledge we have is testimonial; assertion is one of our main epistemic vehicles towards success in inquiry.

Just like hearts were selected for their reliability in generating biological benefit, I submit, the speech act of assertion has been selected for its reliability in generating epistemic benefit, that is, testimonial knowledge.[44] In turn, because it generated testimonial knowledge in our ancestors, assertion enabled them to survive – find out about the whereabouts of dangerous predators, find food and so on – and reproduce, thereby replicating the same practice with the same function in their descendants. The fact that assertion generates testimonial knowledge in hearers explains the continuous existence of the practice. Just like your heart's pumping blood keeps you alive which, in turn, contributes to the explanation of the continuous existence of the heart, the function of assertion is a stabilizing one, for it 'encourages speakers to keep using the device and hearers to keep responding to it with the same (with a stable) response' (Millikan 2005, 94).

Of course, the epistemic function of assertion – that of generating knowledge – need not be, and plausibly is not, the only function of assertion. Assertion, like all actions, also serves prudential functions – plausibly, helping us coordinate with each other – social functions – enabling social bonding, and so on. In turn, the requirements generated by these functions can and often will outweigh the requirements of the epistemic function at particular contexts.

---

[44] For hearer-oriented functionalist accounts of assertion, see Garcia-Carpintero (2004) and Kelp (2018). For an anti-reductionist view of testimonial entitlement replying on a functionalist knowledge account of assertion, see Simion (2021).

Now, recall that functions of a particular type come with associated norms of the corresponding type. When functioning properly, the speech act of assertion will fulfil the epistemic norm constitutively associated with its epistemic e-function of reliably generating testimonial knowledge; it will work the way it is supposed to work, where the right way of working is partly constituted by reliably delivering the epistemic goods in normal conditions.

The question to ask, then, if we want to know the content of the epistemic norm we are after is: how does assertion fulfil its function of generating knowledge in hearers in normal conditions? I submit that the overwhelmingly plausible answer is: by being knowledgeable. First, on most if not all accounts of testimony in the literature,[45] in the vast majority of cases, the speaker needs to know in order to be able to generate knowledge in the hearer. Furthermore, knowledge is all the speaker needs to this effect when it comes to her epistemic standing vis-à-vis p.[46] Also, exceptions to this rule describe extremely unusual scenarios,[47] which renders them highly unlikely to affect the functionalist derivation. To see this, consider driving: norms regulating speed limit within city bounds are presumably there to make it so that we arrive safely at our destination. However, driving 30 mph within city bounds is not *always* the ideal speed; there are instances when, for instance, overtaking at 50 mph will avoid a major accident. Nevertheless, the reason why the norm says, 'Drive at most 30 mph within city bounds!' is because, most of the time, that is the ideal speed for safety purposes. Similarly, since in the vast majority of cases, knowledge on the speaker side is both needed and enough to generate knowledge in hearers, KNA is vindicated: an epistemically proper assertion will be one that, in normal conditions, fulfils its epistemic function of generating knowledge in hearers by being knowledgeable.

Why not a truth function, coupled with a corresponding truth norm? Ruth Millikan (1984) and Peter Graham (2010) defend a view along these lines. I have argued extensively against a truth function in Section 1, I will not rehearse these arguments here. Furthermore, note that, even assuming a truth function, what the etiological machinery bears out is a knowledge norm of

---

[45] See Lackey (2008) for a nice overview.

[46] Williamson (2000, 256) makes a similar point, although he does not pursue this line any further: 'Although there are special cases in which someone comes to know p by hearing someone who does not know p assert p [...], the normal procedure by which the hearer comes to know p requires the speaker to know p too'.

[47] Exceptions are few, and they roughly boil down to two types of cases: first, we have 'selfless asserters', asserting on knowledge-level justification without belief (Lackey 2007). These speakers assert to what is best supported by evidence, although they cannot get themselves to believe it due to some rationality failures. Secondly, we have 'Compulsive Liar' cases (Lackey 2008). Roughly, what happens in these cases is that, although the speaker intends to lie on a regular basis, some external intervention makes it so that she safely asserts the truth.

assertion rather than a truth norm. After all, in virtue of the ready availability of knowledge, plausibly, the way in which assertion fulfils its function of generating a true belief in its audience in normal conditions is by being knowledgeable.

4.3 Assertion, Knowledge, and Context

Here are two very attractive theses: KNA and Classical Invariantism (CI). The former is familiar already. The latter states that knowledge and knowledge attributions are insensitive to practical stakes. Both are borne out by the normative picture defended here. Alas, for the most part, the epistemological literature of the last decade takes KNA and CI to be incompatible. The culprit is the intuitive sensitivity of permissible assertion to practical stakes. Consider the classic cases from Keith DeRose (2002, henceforth 'contextualist cases'):

Bank Case A. My wife and I are driving home on a Friday afternoon. We plan to stop at the bank on the way home to deposit our pay cheques. But as we drive past the bank, we notice that the lines inside are very long, as they often are on Friday afternoons. Although we generally like to deposit our pay cheques as soon as possible, it is not especially important in this case that they be deposited right away, so I suggest that we drive straight home and deposit our pay cheques on Saturday morning. My wife says, 'Maybe the bank won't be open tomorrow. Lots of banks are closed on Saturdays.' I reply, 'No, I know it'll be open. I was just there two weeks ago on Saturday. It's open until noon.'

Bank Case B. My wife and I drive past the bank on a Friday afternoon, as in Case A, and notice the long lines. I again suggest that we deposit our pay cheques on Saturday morning, explaining that I was at the bank on Saturday morning only two weeks ago and discovered that it was open until noon. But in this case, we have just written a very large and very important cheque. If our pay cheques are not deposited into our chequing account before Monday morning, the important cheque we wrote will bounce, leaving us in a very bad situation. And, of course, the bank is not open on Sunday. My wife reminds me of these facts. She then says, 'Banks do change their hours. Do you know the bank will be open tomorrow?' Remaining as confident as I was before that the bank will be open then, still, I reply, 'Well, no, I don't know. I'd better go in and make sure.'

Now, here is the thought behind the incompatibility claim: it seems permissible in Bank Case A, but not in Bank Case B, for DeRose to flat out assert that the bank will be open tomorrow. Thus, permissible assertion seems to require more warrant in high stakes than in low-stakes scenarios. If this is so, the thought goes, we are faced with the following dilemma (henceforth also the 'Shiftiness

Dilemma', or SD): either we embrace KNA but are stuck with a view that takes knowledge/knowledge attribution to be sensitive to practical considerations, or we hold on to classical invariantism, but then we'll have to give up KNA.

According to Williamson, SD is a false dilemma: what explains the normative profile of cases of shiftiness of proper assertability is the fact that the relevant agents lack higher-order knowledge. The thought, roughly, goes as follows: in high-stakes contexts, if you act without *knowing* that you are meeting the conditions for proper action you'll be blameworthy. The case of assertion is an instance of this general principle: since knowledge is the norm for assertion, what's expected from speakers in high-stakes scenarios is that they know that they know before making an assertion. However, according to Williamson, contextualist cases are borderline cases of knowledge and therefore exhibit failure of luminosity.

Consider, however, the following pair of cases due to Jessica Brown:

Lo: [S]uppose that Lo truly believes that the seaweed in front of her is correctly classified as of type F, on the basis of the testimony of an accompanying expert. She has no reason to doubt the expert's competence and the expert is in fact reliable (Brown 2005, 323).

Hi: Hi is in the same epistemic position as Lo; she truly believes that the seaweed in front of her is correctly classified as of type F on the basis of the testimony of an accompanying [reliable] expert [...]. However, [in her context], [...] seaweed F could rapidly come to dominate the local seaweed population, leading to loss of the marine diversity for which the area is internationally renowned. The only way to prevent this loss would be a hugely expensive clean-up programme which would require closure of nearby tourist resorts. Further, in Hi's context, various error possibilities have been raised, such as the possibility that the expert is mistaken ('Experts do sometimes make mistakes') (Brown 2005, 323).

It looks as though in Hi, but not in Lo, it is inappropriate to assert 'The seaweed is of type F' or to rely on the proposition that the seaweed is of type F in, say, deciding whether to close the local resort. Furthermore, it looks as though Hi should make further checks by asking one or more other experts for their opinion.

Note, though, that Lo's warrant is well above the ordinary standards for knowledge, and, as such, not a borderline case exhibiting failure of luminosity. As a result, the unassertability in high-stakes cases cannot be explained in terms of the absence of second-order knowledge in virtue of failure of luminosity.

In response, Williamson ventures to handle such cases by employing contextual variability when it comes to the needed number of iterations of knowledge: the higher the stakes, the higher the order of knowledge required for permissible action. Accordingly, in Brown's cases, in spite of being in a fairly strong epistemic situation, Hi still misses the contextually appropriate number of iterations of knowledge.

There is an important worry for this line of response, however. Recall that the main advantage of Williamson's account is that it is but a special case of a more general phenomenon: again, the idea is that, in general, we tend to harshly judge people who, when a lot is at stake, act without knowing that they meet the condition for proper action. Consider the following case:

Lock. The company you work for operates a norm that the door be locked after 10pm. Moreover, the last employee is in charge with this. Today you are the last employee and you know this. You also know that it's of special importance today that the door is locked as your company just received some valuable goods.

In this case, it's plausible that Williamson is right in that you'll be subject to blame if it turns out that you didn't know that the door was locked after 10pm, even if, as a matter of fact, it was. What is less plausible, however, is that, as the stakes go up, you need further iterations of knowledge. Consider:

*Lock**. The company you work for operates a norm that the door be locked after 10pm. Moreover, the last employee is in charge with this. Today you are the last employee and you know this. You also know that it's of vital importance today that the door is locked. Your company invested all its capital in certain goods that just arrived and are nearly certain to be stolen and result in the company's bankruptcy unless the door is locked.

Here too, it's plausible that you'll be subject to blame if it turns out that you didn't know that the door was locked, even if, as a matter of fact, it was locked. What's less plausible is that you'll be subject to blame if the door is locked and you knew that it is locked, but you didn't know that you knew that the door is locked.

What comes to light, then, is that while in general we legitimately blame those who don't know that they comply with a certain norm, we can't legitimately blame them in cases in which they comply with the norm and know that they do, but don't attain some higher number of iterations for knowledge. But given that the case of assertion was meant to be a special case of the general phenomenon, we'd expect assertion to behave in this way also. By the same token, we have reason to think that the Williamsonian explanation of contextualist cases remains unsuccessful.

Can the functionalist picture do better? I think it can (Simion 2021). Recall that a given trait/artefact/act can have several functions simultaneously, even several functions of different types. Furthermore, there can be situations where the two functions come in conflict, at which point the more stringent requirement will take precedence. In other words, when there is a conflict between the normative requirements associated with two functions, one requirement may override the other and dictate what's the all-things-considered good to observe. We can now take this idea and put it to use for our epistemological purposes. It is highly plausible that the epistemic function is merely one of the many functions served by assertion. One other very important function of assertion, as with action in general, will be a prudential one, serving our practical ends. The epistemic function will, in most cases, complement this prudential function: generating testimonial knowledge in one's hearer with regard to an imminent threat, or about the whereabouts of resources are paradigm cases. However, the two functions can also come into conflict. For instance, even if one knows that one's boss is bald, it may not be polite, prudent, or relevant to point this out to him (Brown 2010, 550): surely, here, the prudential function comes in conflict with the epistemic one. What's more, it is also plausible that the prudential function overrides the epistemic. The result is that although it is epistemically permissible to assert that one's boss is bald to him, it is not all things considered permissible for one to do so.

Finally, the phenomenon of conflict and overriding is precisely what explains the unassertability intuition in high-stakes scenarios: in Bank Case 2, strictly epistemically speaking, if DeRose has memorial knowledge that the bank is open on Saturdays, he is permitted to assert that the bank is open on Saturdays. However, prudential constraints concerning the bouncing cheque come into conflict with these epistemic requirements. They override the epistemic constraint and drive the degree of epistemic support required for all-things-considered permissible assertion up to a point DeRose does not reach. As a result, it will be all-things-considered impermissible for DeRose to assert in this case.[48] Compatibly, knowledge is enough for meeting the epistemic norm of assertion, and remains a (*prima facie*) epistemic reason to assert, even in cases in which overriding norms step in and forbid asserting.

---

[48] Note, once more, that the fact that the degree of epistemic support required for permissible assertion is driven up by the high stakes does not imply an epistemic norm is at work: epistemic norms differ from mere norms with epistemic content – that is, norms affecting the level of epistemic support required – which may well be prudential, moral, and so on.

Conclusion

I have argued here that there is no epistemic norm governing action in general,
although most actions will plausibly be governed by several other norms with
epistemic content – like prudential or moral norms. In order for a particular type of
action to be governed by an epistemic norm, it needs be the case that it serves an
epistemic function. Correspondingly, I have defended *Assertion Functionalism*:
According to this view, knowledge is the norm of assertion in virtue of assertion's
function of generating knowledge in hearers.

5 Practical and Theoretical Reasoning

Introduction

There is no epistemic norm for action; rather, action is governed by other types
of norms – prudential, moral, and so on norms – with epistemic content, in
virtue of its prudential, moral, and so on functions. What about practical
reasoning? Of course, practical reasoning will also serve a prudential function:
that of leading to prudentially good action. In virtue of the latter, it will also be
governed by prudential norms. Compatibly with this, practical reasoning also
serves an epistemic function: generating knowledge of what one ought to do. If
I am right, practical reasoning will be governed by a corresponding epistemic
norm, borne out by this function.

This picture I favour, if right, sharply separates action and practical reasoning
normatively. At the same time, it provides us with an exciting opportunity to
unify reasoning: practical and theoretical reasoning will turn out to be governed
by the same epistemic norm – knowledge – in virtue of serving the same
epistemic function in inquiry: generating knowledge of the conclusion.

5.1 The Epistemic Function and Epistemic Norm of Reasoning

At this stage, it will not come as a surprise that the view I want to defend when it
comes to the epistemic function of reasoning (theoretical and practical) is that it
amounts to generating knowledge.[49] Three reasons in support of this thought:

First, recall that I have argued (Section 1) that the practice of inquiry aims at
generating knowledge: that's its epistemic function. In turn, I have claimed that
moves in practices aim at fulfilling the aim of the practice. Since I take reasoning to be a move in the practice of inquiry, my normative picture straightforwardly delivers a knowledge generating function of reasoning.

Second, recall that Section 2 argued that good belief is knowledgeable belief.
On the assumption that the output of reasoning is a conclusion belief, and since

---

[49] See McHugh and Way (2018) for an account of reasoning as a functional good-making kind.

beliefs ought to be knowledgeable, it follows that the function of reasoning is to generate knowledgeable conclusion beliefs.

Third, note that knowledge meets E-Function for reasoning: instances of reasoning have delivered knowledge in the past (empirically highly plausible), this benefitted us epistemically (value of knowledge thesis), which contributes to the explanation of why we keep engaging in reasoning.

If this is right, we can straightforwardly employ our functionalist machinery to the aim of figuring out what epistemic norm is borne out by this picture. I submit that the overwhelmingly plausible answer, given the easy availability of knowledge, and given that, in the vast majority of instances of reasoning, knowledge of the premises is necessary for achieving knowledge of the conclusion, is that, in normal conditions, reasoning generates knowledge of the conclusion from known premises.[50] If this is right, knowledge is the epistemic norm of reasoning:

KNR: Relying on p as a premise in reasoning is epistemically permissible iff one knows that p.

One important thing to note: when one discusses epistemic norms for reasoning, there are two things one can be talking about: transition epistemic norms – governing how I should handle the premises and move from them to the conclusion – and epistemic norms pertaining to what premises I am allowed to rely on to begin with. The issue this section is concerned with is the latter: what properties need a proposition enjoy in order to be epistemically permissibly employed in reasoning?; and the answer I defend is: it needs to be known.

One question that arises at this point concerns the scope of the knowledge function and knowledge norm claims: are they restricted to theoretical reasoning, or will they apply to practical reasoning as well? The next section develops a unified view of the epistemic function and normativity of practical and theoretical reasoning.

5.2 Practical vs. Theoretical Reasoning

There are notable difficulties in offering a precise recipe for sharply distinguishing practical from theoretical reasoning. One way to go about it is to take theoretical reasoning to be concerned with answering descriptive questions (about matters of fact), while practical reasoning aims at answering normative

---

[50] Some will find it counterintuitive that, in cases of false justified belief, practical reasoning (or assertion, for that matter) is impermissible. Defenders of justification epistemic norms (e.g. Douven 2008, 2009, Lackey 2007) come to mind. I (and others) have defended knowledge norms against these objections at length in several places (e.g. Kelp and Simion 2021): justified false belief delivers blameless rather than permissible practical reasoning (and assertion), on my view.

questions (about what one ought to do).[51] The problem with this straightforward recipe is that it is too simple. Here is why: on one hand, there are such things as normative matters of fact, that is, facts about what one ought to do. Conversely, conclusions of theoretical reasoning carry normative power too: after all, it looks as though, very roughly, proper instances of theoretical reasoning make it permissible to believe their conclusions, while improper instances thereof deliver impermissible conclusion-beliefs. It is tempting, then, to think that theoretical reasoning too attempts to answer a normative question: the question of what one should believe (Moran 2001). Seen in this way, the contrast between practical and theoretical reasoning becomes essentially a contrast in target of normativity: practical reasoning is concerned with answering the question 'what should I do', while theoretical reasoning is concerned with answering the question: 'what should I believe?'[52] Let's call this way to distinguish practical from theoretical reasoning 'the Simple View'.

Some philosophers are disenchanted with the Simple View: they think that there is more to the distinction between practical and theoretical reasoning than the Simple View suggests. In particular, they think that the two forms of reasoning differ not only in their target, but, importantly, also in their consequences: theoretical reasoning produces changes in one's overall set of beliefs, whereas practical reasoning gives rise to intentional action; it is practical not only in its subject matter, but also in its output ((Harman 1986), (Bratman 1987), henceforth also the Complex View).

I sympathize with the Simple View. Here is why: as defenders of the Complex View themselves acknowledge, a better way to describe the consequences of practical reasoning would be to say that deliberation about action generates appropriate intentions insofar as an agent is rational (Korsgaard 1996). After all, many of us display weakness of will. But if that is the case, intention seems to be a contingent consequence of practical reasoning, premised on the agent's rationality. It's a consequence practical reasoning *should* have, rather than one that it essentially has, in virtue of the type of reasoning that it is. After all, we don't want to say that, in cases of weakness of will, no practical reasoning was exercised, in virtue of no intention being generated. To the contrary, what plausibly goes wrong in cases of weakness of will is precisely that an instance of practical reasoning is at work, but the agent fails to form the intention

---

[51] See Wallace (2018) for a nice overview.

[52] According to Hieronymi 2009, in practical reasoning, we answer questions about whether to do this or that, not questions whether we should do this or that. Similar things could be said about belief. I am sceptical about this: it seems that settling the question as to whether to believe, or to act, will amount to settling the question as to whether one should believe, act, in cases in which one intends to believe, act, well. In turn, settling the question as to what to do when does not have any such normative intention does not require practical reasoning at all.

corresponding to its conclusion. In other words, the agent knows what she should do but fails to form the intention to do it.

If so, a more plausible picture is the one outlined by the Simple View. Compatibly, defenders of the Complex View can come back with a weaker proposal, on which they supplement the Simple View with a normative rather than a descriptive claim: on a Revised Complex View, an instance of reasoning will be an instance of practical reasoning just in case its target of application is action, and it *should* deliver a change in intention. I'm not particularly convinced by this version of the Revised Complex View either; after all, we can easily imagine instances of practical reasoning which deliver the result that some intention that I already had was correct; in this case, no change in intention should follow. That being said, I don't need to settle this issue here, more plausible ways to spell out the Complex View are likely available. The view I develop next is perfectly compatible with both the Simple and the Complex View. Indeed, I believe it offers a nice compromise between them.

According to the view I favour, there is no distinction between practical and theoretical reasoning when it comes to the nature of their conclusion-attitudes (as per the Simple View):[53] in both cases, the conclusion is a belief. In line with the Complex View, the difference lies with the *prudential* normative pressure that the conclusion exerts over one's intentions and actions: in the case of practical reason, one's actions and intentions (*prudentially*) should align with the conclusion belief: one (prudentially) should intend to do and do what one believes one ought to do as a result to one's good practical reasoning.

On the picture defended here, good belief is knowledgeable belief. As such, on this picture, in contrast to action, practical reasoning does also serve an epistemic function, on top of its prudential function: generating a good belief – that is, knowledge – of what one ought to do. Note, also, that knowledge meets E-Function: instances of practical reasoning have delivered knowledge of what one ought to do in the past, this benefitted us, which contributes to the explanation of why we keep engaging in practical reasoning. If that is so, practical reasoning will, arguably, afford an epistemic norm.

But is this really *a* function of practical reasoning, one might wonder? Isn't *the* function rather to generate an intention and/or the corresponding action, as the (Revised) Complex View would have it? And if this is so, will it not be the

---

[53] While I have strong sympathies for the Simple View, my account does not hang on it. If it turns out that the Revised Complex View is correct, my view will predict that (1) there is no epistemic norm for practical reasoning, since it doesn't have any epistemic function, and (2) reasoning about what one ought to do is an instance of theoretical reasoning, governed by a knowledge norm.

case that the arguments presented here against there being an epistemic norm for action apply, mutatis mutandis, to practical reasoning too?

A few things about this. First, I accept that practical reasoning does have an important prudential function in generating prudentially proper intentions and actions. This prudential function will generate a prudential norm for practical reasoning. It is not my task here to discuss what the prudential norms for action or practical reasoning might be, I will leave that to practical philosophy to decide. What I am interested in is whether practical reasoning also has an epistemic function – and my answer is yes: to produce epistemically good (knowledgeable) conclusion beliefs. Importantly, the Complex View does not exclude the possibility of practical reasoning *also* generating a conclusion-belief on top of the relevant intention (indeed, the possibility of weakness of will requires there to be something else that plays the role of the conclusion of the relevant instance of practical reasoning; belief seems well qualified to do so).

Second, I worry about a picture on which knowledge of the conclusion has nothing to do with the propriety (of sorts) of practical reasoning, and the latter is only to be assessed in terms of the propriety of the resulting intention. To see why, consider a case in which I reason as follows: 'It's raining outside/If it's raining, I ought to take an umbrella/Therefore, I ought not take an umbrella.' This is a bad instance of reasoning. Now, say that, in spite of my conclusion belief, I go ahead and take the umbrella anyway. A picture on which the prudential function is the only function of practical reasoning – in virtue of its only consequence being the corresponding intention – has trouble explaining what went wrong here. A view like this will have to describe the case earlier as one where two pieces of reasoning are happening; one theoretical (the one with the bad conclusion belief) and one practical (the one with the good conclusion-intention). After all, this view takes the output of the relevant piece of reasoning to determine the nature thereof – theoretical or practical. So what we have earlier on this view is a correct instance of practical reasoning (from it's raining and if it's raining, I ought to take the umbrella to actually forming the intention of taking it and, in fact, taking it) and a bad instance of theoretical reasoning (to the conclusion belief that I ought not take the umbrella). This picture, however, fails to explain the following datum: it looks as though, my taking the umbrella after I reach the (mistaken) conclusion that I ought not do it doesn't make things better, reasoning-wise – if anything, it makes things worse: after all, not only am I a bad reasoner, but my actions and my beliefs also seem to come in conflict with each other.

But couldn't the defender of this view also explain away the intuition of permissibility in this example by appeal to requirements of structural rationality without also assuming further epistemic functions for practical reasoning? The answer, in short, is 'no': the problem doesn't go away if we stipulate that there is no intention to take the umbrella formed in this case, but rather just the corresponding action.

Third, even if it is plausible that the prudential function is *the main* function of practical reasoning, it is perfectly compatible with practical reasoning having a prudential function (generating a prudentially good intention/intentional action) that it *also* has an epistemic function (generating knowledge of what one ought to do). Insofar as an epistemic function is present, an epistemic norm will drop out of it.

If I am right in thinking that theoretical and practical reasoning serve the same epistemic function – generating knowledge of the conclusion – the argument for the norm governing reasoning presented in the previous section will work for practical reasoning as well, mutatis mutandis. What we get, then, is a knowledge norm for practical reasoning.

5.3 Reasoning and Normative Conflict

In virtue of stipulating that epistemically permissible practical reasoning on one hand, and prudentially permissible practical reasoning and action on the other, can come apart, the view allows for normative conflicts at the level of thought, as well as between thought and action. For the former, consider: on my view, in Bank Case B, I am epistemically permitted to reason from *the bank is open on Saturday*. This will result in my affirming propositions like *the best option is to come back tomorrow* and in my making that plan. But prudentially I ought not reason in this way, because it is too risky: if I do, I may well end up performing a prudentially impermissible action. So, it looks as if we can have conflicts of the type: 'epistemically you ought to reason from p but practically you ought not'. I want to say that this is exactly right: to see this, note that the case is similar to other cases of normative conflict in thought. Take, for instance, a case in which I wishfully think that my friends love me. Prudentially this may well be permissible, because it makes me feel happy, and it may well also lead to prudentially permissible action (being nice to my friends). Still, wishful thinking remains epistemically problematic. Conversely, believing that I am the smartest person in the room may well be epistemically permissible (because, say, known) but prudentially problematic (because it gives rise to a disposition to treat others with contempt, and suffer the consequences).

In virtue of the distinction between prudential and epistemic propriety, the view also avoids traditional problems for cognitivist commitments – such as that intentions involve beliefs, that incoherent intentions imply epistemic irrationality, and that epistemic normative requirements explain practical normative requirements. My account does not commit me to any of these, in virtue of its normative divorce between the epistemic and the prudential propriety of practical reason: first, it is perfectly compatible with my view that a prudentially permissible instance of practical reasoning never delivers a conclusion belief (just the conclusion intention). Second, since my view only takes intentions to be subject to prudential rationality, it does not predict epistemic rationality in cases of incoherent intentions – unless, of course, they are associated with corresponding incoherent beliefs. Finally, my account divorces epistemic normative requirements sharply from practical normative requirements, so it need not commit to any of them explaining the other.

How about knowledge-based criticisms of actions in high-stakes cases (McGrath 2015, 143–144)? If it's not epistemic propriety at issue, we would not expect the criticisms of actions in high-stakes cases to mention knowledge. They wouldn't be, 'but you don't know that' or 'but do you know it?' And yet these seem permissible criticisms of actions in high-stakes cases. In particular, if one was trying to question some other form of propriety for which *more than knowledge* is needed, why would one give a knowledge-based challenge?

Knowledge denial data in high stakes have been subject to extensive rebuttals in experimental philosophy (e.g. Feltz & Zarpentine (2010)). Even philosophical intuitions are shaky when it comes to whether knowledge denial criticisms are permissible in high-stakes cases to begin with (Pritchard 2005). Also, the natural soundingness of the following exchange suggests that my view gets the right result here, in that the knowledge-based criticism is rejected, while the certainty-based criticism is accepted: 'Let's not stop today to make the deposit, the bank will be open tomorrow.' 'You don't know that!' 'Yes I do, I've been there two weeks ago on a Saturday and it was open.' 'Still, you can't be sure, banks do change their hours sometimes; let's just stop today.'

A few last things to note: Importantly, the functionalist claim does not imply that knowledge of premises is always necessary for knowledge of the conclusion. After all, functionalist norms do not track necessary conditions for function fulfilment, but merely the most reliable ways to fulfil the corresponding functions in normal conditions. The claim is that reasoning from premises one does not know is always impermissible, although it might, on occasion, lead to function fulfilment.

To see why this an important advantage of the view, consider the following variation of the umbrella case earlier: The probability of rain is .98/If there is a .98 probability of rain, I should take an umbrella/Therefore, I should take the umbrella. Now, say that I'm wrong: the probability of rain is actually .97. Still, intuitively, I know the conclusion: I should take the umbrella.

Consider, also, a corresponding case of knowledge form falsehood (Klein 2008) in the case of theoretical reasoning: Counting with some care the number of people present at my talk, I reason: 'There are 53 people at my talk; therefore my 100 hand-out copies are sufficient.' My premise is false. There are 52 people in attendance – I double counted one person who changed seats during the count. And yet, intuitively, I know my conclusion.

Cases like these are thought by many[54] to be problematic for knowledge norms of practical and, respectively theoretical reasoning. Crucially, they are not problematic for the view defended here: just like hearts can pump blood even when improperly functioning, instances of reasoning can deliver knowledge when improper too. This, however, does not falsify the normative claim that reasoning should always proceed from knowledge.

In further good news, the picture defended here is also compatible with cases of intuitively permissible action (and intention) from (epistemically) bad reasoning. We are fallible creatures: We often rely on heuristics and habits when we act, and, short of disaster, that's perfectly fine: we have limited computing capacities. Also, we may often not even consider the option that corresponds to what we ought to do. We often also get our priorities wrong. We do things in the wrong order. However, we still get everything done (although perhaps with more effort) or at least well enough to avoid disabling disaster. On pain of extreme demandingness, one could argue, knowledge of oughts does not seem needed for permissible action in all walks of life. Note that my view is perfectly compatible with the prudential norm governing practical reasoning (and action) being much weaker than knowledge. All my view requires is that knowledge of the premises be present for the *epistemic* norm of practical reasoning to be met, which, in turn, in normal conditions, will reliably generate epistemic function fulfilment: knowledge of the conclusion. Compatibly, the epistemic norm may well be often overridden by prudential considerations, in which case less than knowledge will be needed for all-things-considered (and prudentially) permissible practical reasoning. That's fine (all-things-considered).

Here are some more questions for a view like mine: first, what does the account say about Buridan-type dilemmas? I ought to get a can of soup. Alas, there are two cans of soup of equal quality in front of me. They are the same price and they are both the same distance from me. I know that I ought to take a can, but that only takes me so far. I don't bring practical reasoning to its conclusion until I know that I ought to get a particular can, but I know that there's no particular can that I ought to take, so I know that I can't know that I ought to take this can rather than that one.

---

[54] Weisberg (2013).

Second, what does the account say about unknowable obligations, and how they fit with the need for action? I might know that I'll never know whether I ought to choose A or ought to choose B, but the need to resolve a practical question using practical reasoning doesn't go away in the way that, say, the need to engage in theoretical reasoning goes away when I know that I can't know the answer to some salient question.

Again, my view, in contrast to all other knowledge-based views of the normativity of practical reasoning, does not have these problems: the view does predict that no epistemically permissible practical reasoning is available in these cases. Compatibly, however, one can act prudentially permissibly, since knowledge is not necessary for *prudentially* permissible practical reasoning. As such, whatever the correct way to deal with these cases, prudentially speaking, turns out to be, my view can accommodate it.

There is one last worry I would like to address: Why should we assume that practical reasoning also has an epistemic function, in addition to its practical (/moral, etc.) one to begin with? Can't we explain everything we need to explain by assuming that practical reasoning is governed by a prudential knowledge norm? Couldn't its prudential function alone explain why one is permitted to use p as a premise in practical reasoning if and only if one knows p? For instance, couldn't it be the case that reasoning and forming intentions only on the basis of knowledge would guarantee better practical results in the long run and safer achievements (Fassio 2017)?

Importantly, my view is compatible with a view according to which, for example, the prudential function of action and practical reasoning also predicts that knowledge is the prudential norm for action and practical reasoning, sourced in their prudential function. If this turns out to be the case, on my view, the epistemic and prudential norm will just happen to have the same content, in virtue of the same condition being reliably conducive to, for example, both the relevant prudential goods/function fulfilment and the relevant epistemic goods/function fulfilment. However, my view also has the flexibility to allow that this is not the case, and thus to explain, at the same time, cases put forth in the literature in support of a knowledge norm, as well as cases put forth to show that knowledge is too strong a norm for some cases (e.g. umbrella cases) and too weak for others (e.g. high-stakes cases): it can do so by allowing variability in the prudential norm, while, at the same time, keeping the content of the epistemic norm fixed.

Conclusion

This section proposed a picture on which action and practical reasoning are, epistemically, normative strangers: they share a prudential function, but not an epistemic function; as such, they are both governed by prudential norms, but the latter, and not the former, is also governed by an epistemic norm in virtue of its epistemic function of generating knowledge of what one ought to do. Excitingly, though, this picture unifies the epistemic normativity of reasoning: practical and theoretical reasoning share epistemic norm in virtue of sharing epistemic function: generating knowledge of the conclusion.

References

Beddor, B. (2020). New Work for Certainty. *Philosophers' Imprint*, 20(8): 1–25.

Benton, M. (2011). Two More for the Knowledge Account of Assertion. *Analysis*, 71: 684–687.

Benton, M. (2014). Knowledge Norms. *Internet Encyclopedia of Philosophy*. https://iep.utm.edu/kn-norms/

Bird, A. (2007). Justified Judging. *Philosophy and Phenomenological Research*, 74: 81–110.

Bird, A. (2010). Social Knowing. *Philosophical Perspectives*, 24: 23–56.

Bird, A. (2022). *Knowing Science*. Oxford: Oxford University Press.

Blome-Tillmann, M. (2017). 'More Likely than Not' – Knowledge First and the Role of Bare Statistical Evidence in Courts of Law. In A. Carter, E. Gordon, and B. Jarvis (eds.), *Knowledge First: Approaches in Epistemology and Mind*, 278–292. Oxford: Oxford University Press.

Boholm, M., McColler, N., and Hansson, S. O. (2016). The Concepts of Risk, Safety and Security: Applications in Everyday Language. *Risk Analysis*, 36(2): 320–338.

BonJour, L. (1980). Externalist Theories of Empirical Knowledge. *Midwest Studies in Philosophy*, 5: 53–73.

BonJour, L. (1985). *The Structure of Empirical Knowledge*. Cambridge, MA: Harvard University Press.

Bratman, M. E. (1981). Intention and Means-End Reasoning. *The Philosophical Review*, 90(2): 252–265.

Brown, J. (2005). Williamson on Luminosity and Contextualism. *The Philosophical Quarterly*, 55(219): 319–327.

Brown, J. (2008). Subject-Sensitive Invariantism and the Knowledge Norm for Practical Reasoning. *Noûs*, 42(2008): 167–189.

Brown, J. (2010). Knowledge and Assertion. *Philosophy and Phenomenological Research*, 81: 549–566.

Brown, J. (2011). Assertion and Practical Reasoning: Common or Divergent Epistemic Standards? *Philosophy and Phenomenological Research*, 84(1): 123–157.

Brown, J. (2018). *Fallibilism: Evidence and Knowledge*. Oxford: Oxford University Press.

Buller, D. J. (1998). Etiological Theories of Function: A Geographical Survey. *Biology and Philosophy*, 13(4): 505–527.

Burge, T. (1993). Content Preservation. *Philosophical Review*, 102(4): 457–488.

Burge, T. (2003). Perceptual Entitlement. *Philosophy and Phenomenological Research*, 67(3): 503–548.

Carter, J. A. and Pritchard, D. (2015). Knowledge-How and Cognitive Achievement. *Philosophy and Phenomenological Research*, 91(1): 181–199.

Carter, A. and Miracchi, L. (2024). What the Tortoise Should Do: A Knowledge-First Virtue Approach to the Basing Relation. *Nous*, 58(2): 456–481.

Choi, S. and Fara, M. (2018). Dispositions. In E. N. Zalta (ed.), *The Stanford Encyclopedia of Philosophy* (Fall 2018 Edition). https://plato.stanford.edu/archives/fall2018/entries/dispositions/.

Cohen, S. (1986). Knowledge and Context. *The Journal of Philosophy*, 83: 574–583.

Cummins, R. (1975). Functional Analysis. *The Journal of Philosophy*, 72(20): 741–765.

DeRose, K. (2002). Assertion, Knowledge, and Context. *Philosophical Review*, 111: 167–203.

Douven, I. (2008). Knowledge and Practical Reasoning. *Dialectica*, 62(1): 101–118.

Douven, I. (2009). Assertion, Moore and Bayes. *Philosophical Studies*, 144: 361–375.

Douven, I. and Williamson, T. (2006). Generalizing the Lottery Paradox. *British Journal for the Philosophy of Science*, 57 (4): 755–779.

Dutant, J. and Littlejohn, C. (2021). Defeaters as Indicators of Ignorance. In J. Brown and M. Simion (eds.), *Reasons, Justification, and Defeat*. Oxford: Oxford University Press.

Elgin, C. Z. (2017). *True Enough*. Cambridge: MIT Press.

van Elswyk, P. and Willard-Kyle, C. (Forthcoming). Hedging and the Norm of Belief, *Australasian Journal of Philosophy*.

Falbo, A. (2023). Inquiring Minds Want to Improve. *Australasian Journal of Philosophy*, 101(2): 298–312.

Fantl, J. and McGrath, M. (2002). Evidence, Pragmatics and Justification. *Philosophical Review*, 111(1): 67–94.

Fantl, J. and McGrath, M. (2009). *Knowledge in an Uncertain World*. Oxford: Oxford University Press.

Fassio, D. (2017). Is There an Epistemic Norm of Practical Reasoning? *Philosophical Studies*, 174: 2137–2166.

Feltz, A. and Zarpentine, C. (2010). Do You Know More When It Matters Less? *Philosophical Psychology*, 23(5): 683–706.

Friedman, J. (2020). The Epistemic and the Zetetic. *Philosophical Review*, 129(4): 501–536.

Garcia-Carpintero, M. (2004). Assertion and the Semantics of Force-Markers. In C. Bianchi (ed.), *The Semantics/Pragmatics Distinction*, 133–166. CSLI.

Geach, P. (1956). Good and Evil. *Analysis*, 17: 33–42.

Gerken, M. (2011). Warrant and Action. *Synthese*, 178(3): 529–547.

Gerken, M. (2014). Same, Same but Different: The Epistemic Norms of Assertion, Action, and Practical Reasoning. *Philosophical Studies*, 168: 725–744.

Gerken, M. (2018). Against Knowledge-First Epistemology. In E. Gordon, B. Jarvis, and A. Carter (eds.), *Knowledge-First Approaches in Epistemology and Mind*, 46–71. Oxford: Oxford University Press.

Gettier, E. (1963). Is Justified True Belief Knowledge? *Analysis*, 23: 121–123.

Gibbons, J. (2013). *The Norm of Belief*. Oxford: Oxford University Press.

Goldberg, S. (2015). *Assertion: The Philosophical Significance of a Speech Act*. Oxford: Oxford University Press.

Goldberg, S. (2016). On the Epistemic Significance of Evidence You Should Have Had. *Episteme*, 13(4): 449–470.

Goldberg, S. (2018). *To the Best of Our Knowledge: Social Expectations and Epistemic Normativity*. Oxford, UK: Oxford University Press.

Goldman, A. (1976). Discrimination and Perceptual Knowledge. *The Journal of Philosophy*, 73(20): 771–791.

Goldman, A. (1988). Strong and Weak Justification. *Philosophical Perspectives*, 2: 51–69.

Goodman, J. and Salow, B. (2018). Taking a Chance on KK. *Philosophical Studies*, 175(1): 183–196.

Graham, P. J. (2008). Testimonial Entitlement and the Function of Comprehension. In D. Pritchard, A. Millar, and A. Haddock (eds.), *Social Epistemology*, 148–174. Oxford, GB: Oxford University Press.

Graham, P. J. (2012). Epistemic Entitlement. *Nous*, 46(3): 449–482.

Graham, P. J. (2014). Functions, Warrant, History. In A. Fairweather and O. Flanagan (eds.), *Naturalizing Epistemic Virtue*, 15–35. Cambridge: Cambridge University Press.

Grice, P. (1989). *Studies in the Way of Words*. Cambridge, MA: Harvard University Press.

Harman, G. (1986). *Change in View: Principles of Reasoning*, Cambridge, MA: The MIT Press.

Hawthorne, J. (2004). *Knowledge and Lotteries*. Oxford: Oxford University Press.

Hawthorne, J. and Srinivasan, A. (2013). Disagreement without Transparency: Some Bleak Thoughts. In D. Christensen and J. Lackey (eds.), *The Epistemology of Disagreement: New Essays*, 9–30. Oxford: Oxford University Press.

Hawthorne, J. and Stanley, J. (2008). Knowledge and Action. *Journal of Philosophy*, 105(10): 571–590.

Hetherington, S. (2002). Epistemic Responsibility: A Dilemma. *The Monist*, 85(3): 398–414.

Hetherington, S. (2022). *Defining Knowledge*. Cambridge: Cambridge University Press.

Hieronimy, P. (2009). The Will as Reason. *Philosophical Perspectives*, 23(1): 201–220.

Ichikawa, J. J. (2014). Justification Is Potential Knowledge. *Canadian Journal of Philosophy*, 44(2): 184–206.

Kearl, T. and Willard-Kyle, C. (Forthcoming). Epistemic Cans. *Philosophy and Phenomenological Research*.

Kelp, C. (2014a). Two for the Knowledge Goal of Inquiry. *American Philosophical Quarterly*, 51, 227–232.

Kelp, C. (2014b). No Justification for Lottery Losers. *Pacific Philosophical Quarterly*, 95: 205–217.

Kelp, C. (2015). Understanding Phenomena. *Synthese*, 192: 3799–3816.

Kelp, C. (2016). Assertion: A Function First Account. *Noûs*, 5(2): 411–442. Online First.

Kelp, C. (2018). Assertion: A Function First Account. *Noûs*, 52(2): 411–442.

Kelp, C. (2021). *Inquiry, Knowledge, and Understanding*. Oxford: Oxford University Press.

Kelp, C. (2023). *The Nature and Normativity of Defeat*. Cambridge Elements Series. Cambridge.

Kelp, C. and Simion, M. (2017). Commodious Knowledge. *Synthese*, 194(5): 1487–1502.

Kelp, C. and Simion, M. (2021). *Sharing Knowledge: A Functionalist Account of Assertion*. Cambridge: Cambridge University Press.

Kelp, C. and Simion, M. (2024). Justification as the Proper Route to Knowledge. MS.

Khalifa, K. (2017). *Understanding, Explanation, and Scientific Knowledge*. Cambridge: Cambridge University Press.

Klein, P. (2008). Useful False Beliefs. In S. Quentin (ed.), *Epistemology: New Essays*, 25–61. Oxford: Oxford University Press.

Korsgaard, C. (1986). Skepticism about Practical Reason. *The Journal of Philosophy*, 83(1): 5–25; reprinted in Korsgaard, C. (1996). *Creating the Kingdom of Ends*, 311–334. Cambridge: Cambridge University Press.
(1996). *The Sources of Normativity*. Cambridge: Cambridge University Press.

Kotzen, M. (2019). A Formal Account of Evidential Defeat. In B. Fitelson, R. Borges, and C. Braden (eds.), *Themes from Klein: Knowledge, Scepticism, and Justification*, 213–234. Synthese Library.

Kvanvig, J. (2003). *The Value of Knowledge and the Pursuit of Understanding*. Cambridge: Cambridge University Press.

Lackey, J. (2007). Norms of Assertion. *Noûs*, 41: 594–626.

Lackey, J. (2008). Learning from Words. Oxford: Oxford University Press.

Lackey, J. (2018). Duty to Object. *Philosophy and Phenomenological Research*, 101(1): 35–60. Online First.

Lasonen-Aarnio, M. (2014). Higher-Order Evidence and the Limits of Defeat. *Philosophy and Phenomenological Research*, 88(2): 314–345.

Lasonen-Aarnio, M. (MS). *Feasible Dispositions: A Normative Framework*. Oxford: Oxford University Press.

Littlejohn, C. (2013). The Russellian Retreat. *Proceedings of the Aristotelian Society*, 113(3): 293–320.

Littlejohn, C. (2017). Truth, Knowledge, and the Standard of Proof in Criminal Law. *Synthese*, 197(12): 5253–5286.

Littlejohn, C. (Forthcoming). A Plea for Epistemic Excuses. In F. Dorsch and J. Dutant (eds.), *The New Evil Demon*. Oxford: Oxford University Press.

Littlejohn, C. and Turri, J. (2014). *Epistemic Norms*. Oxford: Oxford University Press.

Lord, E. (2018). *The Importance of Being Rational*. Oxford: Oxford University Press.

Maitra, I. (2011). Assertion, Norms and Games. In J. Brown and H. Cappelen (eds.), *Assertion: New Philosophical Essays*, 277–296. Oxford: Oxford University Press.

McGlynn, A. (2014). *Knowledge First?* Palgrave McMillan.

McGlynn, A. (2024a). Known Unknowns and the Limits of Knowledge. In M. Steup, B. Roeber, J. Turri, and E. Sosa (eds.), *Contemporary Debates in Epistemology*, Volume 3, 7–14. New York: Wiley-Blackwell.

McGlynn, A. (2024b). Circumstantial Luck and Knowledge-First Epistemology. In M. Steup, B. Roeber, J. Turri, and E. Sosa (eds.), *Contemporary Debates in Epistemology*, Volume 3, 16–19. Wiley-Blackwell.

McGrath, M. (2015). Two Purposes of Knowledge Attribution and the Contextualism Debate. In J. Greco and D. K. Henderson (eds.), *Epistemic Evaluation: Purposeful Epistemology*, 138–156. Oxford: Oxford University Press.

McHugh, C. (2012). The Truth Norm of Belief. *Pacific Philosophical Quarterly*, 93(1): 8–30.

McHugh, C. and Way, J. (2018). What is Good Reasoning? *Philosophy and Phenomenological Research*, 153–174.

Millar, A. (2010). Knowledge and Recognition. In D. Pritchard, A. Millar, and A. Haddock (eds.), *The Nature and Value of Knowledge: Three Investigations*. Oxford: Oxford University Press.

Millar, A. (2011). Why Knowledge Matters. *Aristotelian Society Supplementary Volume*, 85(1): 63–81.

Millikan, R. (1984). *Language, Thought, and Other Biological Categories*. Cambridge, MA: The MIT Press.

Millikan, R. G. (2004). *Varieties of Meaning*. Cambridge, MA: The MIT Press.

Miracchi, L. (2015). Competence to Know. *Philosophical Studies*, 172 (1): 29–56.

Miracchi, L. (2017). When Evidence Isn't Enough: Suspension, Evidentialism, and Knowledge-First Virtue Epistemology. *Episteme*, 16(4): 413–437.

Miracchi, L. (Forthcoming). Competent Perspectives and the New Evil Demon Problem. In Julien Dutant (ed.), *The New Evil Demon: New Essays on Knowledge, Justification and Rationality*. Oxford: Oxford University Press.

Mona, S. and Kelp, C. (2015). The Tertiary Value Problem and the Superiority of Knowledge. *American Philosophical Quarterly*, 53(4): 397–410.

Montminy, M. (2012). Why Assertion and Practical Reasoning Must Be Governed by the Same Epistemic Norm. *Pacific Philosophical Quarterly*, 93(4): 57–68.

Moore, G. E. (1993). *Principia Ethica* (Revised Edition). Cambridge: Cambridge University Press.

Moran, R. (2001). *Authority and Estrangement: An Essay on Self-Knowledge*. Princeton: Princeton University Press.

Moss, S. (2019). Knowledge and Legal Proof. *Oxford Studies in Epistemology*, 7(2023): 176–213.

Nado, J. (2019). Who Wants to Know? In T. Gendler and J. Hawthorne (eds.), *Oxford Studies in Epistemology*, 114–136. Oxford: Oxford University Press.

Neander, K. (1991). The Teleological Notion of Function. *Australasian Journal of Philosophy*, 69: 454–468.

Pavese, C. (2015). Practical Senses. *Philosophers' Imprint*, 15(29): 1–25.

Plantinga, A. (1993). *Warrant and Proper Function*. New York: Oxford University Press.

Pritchard, D. (2005). *Epistemic Luck*. Oxford: Oxford University Press.

Pritchard, D. (2009). The Value of Knowledge. *The Harvard Review of Philosophy*, 16(1): 86–103.

Pritchard, D. (2015). Risk. *Metaphilosophy* 46(3): 436–461.

Pritchard, D., Miller, A., and Haddock, A. (eds.) (2010). *The Nature and Value of Knowledge*. Oxford: Oxford University Press.

Putnam, H. (1975). The Meaning of Meaning. In *Mind, Language and Reality; Philosophical Papers Volume 2*, 215–271. Cambridge: Cambridge University Press.

Putnam, H. (1982). *Reason, Truth and History*. Cambridge: Cambridge University Press.

Reynolds, S. (2002). Testimony, Knowledge, and Epistemic Goals. *Philosophical Studies*, 110: 139–161.

Reynolds, S. (2013). Justification as the Appearance of Knowledge. *Philosophical Studies*, 163: 367–383.

Roeber, B. (2020). How to Argue for Pragmatic Encroachment. *Synthese*, 197: 2649–2664. https://doi.org/10.1007/s11229-018-1850-4.

Roeber, B. (2018b). The Pragmatic Encroachment Debate. *Nous*, 52(1): 171–195.

Rudy-Hiller, F. (2018). The Epistemic Condition for Moral Responsibility. In E. N. Zalta (ed.), *The Stanford Encyclopedia of Philosophy* (Fall 2018 Edition). https://plato.stanford.edu/archives/fall2018/entries/moral-responsi bility-epistemic/.

Rysiew, P. (2001). The Context-Sensitivity of Knowledge Attributions. *Noûs*, 35(4): 477–514.

Schellenberg, S. (2018). *The Unity of Perception: Content, Consciousness, Evidence*. Oxford: Oxford University Press.

Schnurr, J. (2017). *The Unruly Mind: Against Doxastic Normativism*. DPhil Thesis, Oxford University. https://ora.ox.ac.uk/objects/uuid:c0aa4d1f-780c-43c3-a013-a0bdad9a2454/files/m7cdac4fb763a68e438552d5a3011b2a7.

Schroeder, M. (2012). Value Theory. In E. N. Zalta (ed.), *The Stanford Encyclopedia of Philosophy* (Summer 2012 Edition). http://plato.stanford .edu/archives/sum2012/entries/value-theory/.

Simion, M. (2016). Assertion: Knowledge Is Enough. *Synthese*, 193(10): 3041–3056.

Simion, M. (2018a). Assertion: The Context Sensitivity Dilemma. *Mind & Language*, 34(4): 503–517.

Simion, M. (2018b). A Puzzle for Epistemic WAMs. *Synthese*, 196(11): 4679–4689. Online First.

Simion, M. (2018c). No Epistemic Norm for Action. *American Philosophical Quarterly*, 55(3): 231–238.

Simion, M. (2018d). Epistemic Trouble for Engineering 'Woman'. *Logos and Episteme*, 9(1): 91–98.

Simion, M. (2019). Knowledge-First Functionalism. *Philosophical Issues*, 29(1): 254–267.

Simion, M. (2021). *Shifty Speech and Independent Thought*. Oxford: Oxford University Press.

Simion, M., Kelp, C., and Ghijsen, H. (2016). Norms of Belief. *Philosophical Issues*, 26(1): 375–392.

Simion, M. (2024a). Knowledge Comes First. In M. Steup, B. Roeber, J. Turri, and E. Sosa (eds.), *Contemporary Debates in Epistemology*, Volume 3, 1–7. Wiley-Blackwell.

Simion, M. (2024b). Knowledge Still Comes First. In M. Steup, B. Roeber, J. Turri, and E. Sosa (eds.), *Contemporary Debates in Epistemology*, Volume 3, 14–16. Wiley-Blackwell.

Simion, M. (2024c). Resistance to Evidence and the Duty to Believe. *Philosophy and Phenomenological Research*, 108(1): 203–216.

Simion, M. (2024d). *Resistance to Evidence*. Cambridge: Cambridge University Press.

Simion, M., Kelp, C., and Carter, A. (2022). On Behalf of Knowledge-First Collective Epistemology. In P. Silva and L. Oliveira (eds.), *Doxastic and Propositional Warrant*. London: Routledge.

Sliwa, P. (2017). Moral Understanding as Knowing Right from Wrong. *Ethics*, 127(3): 521–552.

Slote, M. (1989). *Beyond Optimizing*. Cambridge, MA: Harvard University Press.

Sosa, E. (1993). Proper Functionalism and Virtue Epistemology. *Nous*, 27: 51–65.

Sosa, E. (2010). Value Matters in Epistemology. *Journal of Philosophy*, 107: 167–190.

Sosa, E. (2011). *Knowing Full Well*. Princeton: Princeton University Press.

Sosa, E. (2021). *Epistemic Explanations: A Theory of Telic Normativity, and What It Explains*. Oxford: Oxford University Press.

Sperber, D. (2001). An Evolutionary Perspective on Testimony and Argumentation. *Philosophical Topics*, 29: 401–413.

Staffel, J. (Forthcoming). *Unfinished Business. Rational Attitudes in Reasoning*. Oxford: Oxford University Press.

Stanley, J. (2005). *Knowledge and Practical Interests*. Oxford: Oxford University Press.

Stanley, J. and Williamson, T. (2001). Knowing How. *The Journal of Philosophy*, 98(8): 411–444.

Sullivan-Bissett, E. (2017). Biological Function and Epistemic Normativity. *Philosophical Explorations*, 20(1): 94–110.

Sutton, J. (2005). Stick to What You Know. *Noûs*, 39: 359–396.

Tognazzini, N. and Coates, D. J. (2018). Blame. In E. N. Zalta (ed.), *The Stanford Encyclopedia of Philosophy* (Fall 2018 Edition). https://plato.stan ford.edu/archives/fall2018/entries/blame/.

Turri, J. (2010). On the Relationship between Propositional and Doxastic Justification. *Philosophy and Phenomenological Research*, LXXX(2): 312–326.

Turri, J. (2016). The Point of Assertion Is to Transmit Knowledge. *Analysis*, 76(2): 130–136.

Unger, P. (1975). *Ignorance: A Case for Scepticism*. Oxford: Oxford University Press.

Wallace, R. J. (2018). Practical Reason. In E. N. Zalta (ed.), *The Stanford Encyclopedia of Philosophy* (Spring 2018 Edition). https://plato.stanford .edu/archives/spr2018/entries/practical-reason/.

Weiner, M. (2005). Must We Know What We Say? *Philosophical Review*, 114: 227– 251.

Weisberg, J. (2013). Knowledge in Action. *Philosophers' Imprint*, 13: 1–23.

Whiting, D. (2013). Stick to the Facts: On the Norms of Assertion. *Erkenntnis*, 78: 847–867.

Willard-Kyle, C. (2023). The Knowledge Norm for Inquiry. *Journal of Philosophy*, 120(11): 615–640.

Williamson, T. (1996). Knowing and Asserting. *Philosophical Review*, 105(4): 489–523.

Williamson, T. (2000). *Knowledge and Its Limits*. Oxford: Oxford University Press.

Williamson, T. (2005). Knowledge, Context and the Agent's Point of View. In G. Preyer and G. Peter (eds.), *Contextualism in Philosophy: Knowledge, Meaning and Truth*, 91–114. Oxford: Oxford University Press.

Williamson, T. (Forthcoming). Justifications, Excuses, and Sceptical Scenarios. In F. Dorsch and J. Dutant (eds.), *The New Evil Demon*. Oxford: Oxford University Press.

Woodard, E. (Forthcoming). Why Double Check? *Episteme*, 1–24.

Zimmerman, M. J. (1979). Moral Responsibility and Ignorance. *Ethics*, 107(3): 410–426.

Zimmerman, M. (1997). Moral Responsibility and Ignorance. *Ethics*, CVII(3): 410–426.

Acknowledgements

Many thanks to all my philosophy friends for all the support for this research. In particular, many thanks to Tim Williamson for his inspiring work and extraordinary support over the years. Special thanks also go to Jessica Brown, Herman Cappelen, Adam Carter, Sandy Goldberg, Peter Graham, John Greco, Patrick Greenough, Maria Lasonen-Aarnio, Clayton Littlejohn, Chris Kelp, Jennifer Lackey, Aidan McGlynn, Matt McGrath, Lisa Miracchi, Carlotta Pavese, Susanna Schellenberg, and Ernie Sosa.

At some junctures, arguments in this Element draw on and further develop arguments in previously published work: most centrally, my exchange with Aidan McGlynn in *the Contemporary Debates in Epistemology*, 3rd Edition; my 'No Epistemic Norm for Action' (2016, *American Philosophical Quarterly*); my 2019 Norms of Belief in *Philosophical Issues* (co-authored with C. Kelp and H, Ghijsen); and my Knowledge and Reasoning in *Synthese* (2020). Many thanks to the editors of and referees for these venues for all the support.

Many thanks also to Stephen Hetherington, and two anonymous referees for Cambridge University Press, for the extraordinary amount of work in supporting this project.

This project has received funding from the European Research Council (ERC) under the European Union's Horizon 2020 research and innovation programme (KnowledgeLab: Knowledge-First Social Epistemology project, grant agreement No 948356).

Cambridge Elements ☰

Epistemology

Stephen Hetherington

University of New South Wales, Sydney

Stephen Hetherington is Professor Emeritus of Philosophy at the University of New South Wales, Sydney. He is the author of numerous books, including *Knowledge and the Gettier Problem* (Cambridge University Press, 2016), and *What Is Epistemology?* (Polity, 2019), and is the editor of several others, including *Knowledge in Contemporary Epistemology* (with Markos Valaris: Bloomsbury, 2019), and *What the Ancients Offer to Contemporary Epistemology* (with Nicholas D. Smith: Routledge, 2020). He was the Editor-in-Chief of the Australasian Journal of Philosophy from 2013 until 2022.

About the Series

This Elements series seeks to cover all aspects of a rapidly evolving field, including emerging and evolving topics such as: fallibilism; knowing how; self-knowledge; knowledge of morality; knowledge and injustice; formal epistemology; knowledge and religion; scientific knowledge; collective epistemology; applied epistemology; virtue epistemology; wisdom. The series demonstrates the liveliness and diversity of the field, while also pointing to new areas of investigation.

For EU product safety concerns, contact us at Calle de José Abascal, 56–1°,
28003 Madrid, Spain or eugpsr@cambridge.org.